FITTING IN

THINGS MY MOTHER GAVE ME

Aspergers • Crippling Shyness • Introversion • Loneliness • Good Genes • A bit of Polish Jew • Self-containment • Guilt • Manic Depression • LOTS more Loneliness • More Guilt • Lies • An Old Man with a White Beard up in the sky who was watching EVERYTHING I did and didn't like ANY of it • More Lies and a father who was thrown away when I was a baby because he was "A nasty fat man who didn't like children so I sent him away."

And then, when I was eleven, she got me a step-father who I think she found at the back of an old cupboard and who thought everyone under the age of fifty was a criminal. The last time I saw him, over thirty years ago, he was standing on the lawn of their cottage. I think he had taken root and is probably still there shedding acorns.

She also gave me something which, as far as I can tell, I am the ONLY man in the world to have and that is the never-failing ability to put the toilet seat down afterwards.

COLIN THOMPSON

JKP

Everything in this book is true. Some of it is seen through rose-tinted glasses, some of it through dirty windows grey with smoke and tears and cobwebs, but all of it happened. Things are not necessarily in the order they happened, because where they are just seems to be the right place for them. You might think some things are just too unbelievable or funny or silly to be true, but every tiny detail really did happen.

The beginning is not the beginning. It is the first page because I really like the first sentence and I want it to be the first one in this book.

Deya – Mallorca 1968

I was sitting on the terrace of Robert Graves' house with his wife Beryl. 'Remember this,' Beryl said. 'One day this will be your Good Old Days.'
I used to wish that Beryl had been my mother.*

---

* *Over the years there were several people I wished were my mother. My mother was never one of them.*

FOREWORD

The term Asperger's syndrome describes someone who has a different way of perceiving, thinking, learning and relating. This can lead to remarkable creativity and talent in fine art, imagination and sense of humour. Colin Thompson exemplifies all of these qualities. His autobiography is engaging and informative, but is also itself a work of art. As you read his autobiography, you will be enthralled by his abilities as an artist, gain insight into the world as experienced by someone who has Asperger's syndrome, and also enjoy his great sense of humour.

Tony Attwood

My Family Tree.
Not so much a fine
Old English Oak as a copse
of mixed provenance.

ADMIT ONE
KEEP THIS COUPON

LOADING
65%

1968 – OVER THE HILLS AND...

When I was twenty-four we went to live in the eighteenth century.

We travelled there by van, a very cheap old sort of furniture van, hired for the single job of taking us and our sort of furniture away from London – six hundred miles north by road, fifty-three point seven miles west by sea and a final twenty-five point nine miles by road to the far, far away extreme west of the Outer Hebrides.

We were so happy to discover the world wasn't flat even when you went to the very edge. That night, the sea loch next to our house froze over and in the morning when the tide went out it left big sheets of ice draped over the rocks.

We had taken a time machine to another world and another age.

The next day, my oldest friend Mike, who had driven the van, took it back on the ferry to the twentieth century, leaving me, my very, very pregnant second wife Heather and a dog from Shepherd's Bush market ready for the next bit of our Good Old Days. The day after that an ambulance took my wife back across the island to Stornoway Hospital, where she was told to go into labour for almost twenty-four hours and Hannah, the 0.99 per cent person who had been conceived in Mallorca and seemed so huge, came reluctantly into the world, very small and as white as a china doll with her mother's red hair that she could eventually sit on.

So there were three of us and the dog in the croft house with its own tiny beach we had bought for £400 that I had borrowed from Robert Graves with the instructions to pay him back 'when it rained gold'.

Robert had given us another instruction – that we should call our son Danté. Except our new son hadn't been paying attention when Robert had spun Heather's wedding ring on a long red hair over her stomach and the one-hundred per cent guaranteed boy was a girl and so not Danté, but Hannah. Nor was her sister Alice twenty months later.

We grew potatoes and caught fish and mussels and backache and chickens with a rooster who died of a broken ego, but left us with some tiny

chicks who had to live in the kitchen because the weather was unimaginable unless you lived in the Outer Hebrides, which we did.

So we learned to lean on the wind and not fall over.

And we all grew a little bit older and maybe wiser and the eighteenth century was mostly wonderful with early Bob Dylan albums, weak black and white TV with only one station and no phone, until two years later they finally put up the ten telegraph poles we needed, and no road to the house, until we finished spreading the two hundred metres of rock with shovels and a bit of dynamite and more backache, and a very old Renault 4 with the doors fallen off, which forever refused to die, even when we tried to burn it and buried it beneath a five tonne rock and covered it with earth.

And then, several light years away from real life, with a baby and a dog, we finally remembered something we should not have forgotten. We had almost no money and absolutely no way of making any.

We did have a piece of paper and a pen though, so we wrote down all the ways we could think of to make a living on a very little remote Scottish island.

It was not a long list and as we got to know the Hebridean weather the list got a lot shorter. We crossed out all the jobs that involved going out of doors.

So we chose the most obvious one.

We became weavers, not from any arty-crafty love of weaving, but because the Outer Hebrides is where Harris Tweed is made. We bought a second-hand loom for £80 and an old weaver taught us what to do and every second week or so the mills in Stornoway brought us work. Every other week we had to get the dole.

The Harris Tweed loom has no motor. It's the regulations and is like riding a very heavy bicycle underwater and the week we made the tweed we had one pound more than the week we got the dole. This was not a career with any prospects, beyond exceptional thigh muscles.

I drew this picture a couple of years later and probably made more
money selling prints of it than I ever did weaving.

After two years we went back to our list.

We crossed out idea after idea until there was
only one left.

Pottery – this also not from any arty-crafty love
of ceramics, but because it seemed like quite a good
idea, or at least a better idea than any of the others,
and it looked quite easy.

'How hard can it be?' we said as we read our
way through the Penguin *Making Pottery* book.

It did look pretty easy, especially when I thought
about the people I'd seen at art school making
pottery, who were obviously not very bright or they
would have been doing fine art like I was.

So we worked out what we needed and made a list and then found out we could get development grants to create jobs in the remote bits of Scotland and we persuaded our bank to lend us the same amount of money.

We even got a grant of £400 to blow up rocks and build the road to our house. So we bought two electric potter's wheels, because my thighs still hadn't recovered from weaving the tweed, two electric kilns and bags and sacks and jars of all sorts of stuff that looked like it might either be very useful or interesting.

Then we set to work.

And that was when we discovered the secret the book had not told us about.

Making pottery is really, really difficult.

But I did get quite good at shooting, as the bottom of our garden became littered with the remains of all the pots I stood on our fence posts and shot to bits with my BSA rifle.

We bought another book about pottery, but all that one taught us was that lots of potters are very pretentious and all their glazes have Japanese names. We named our glazes after birds with nice names and appropriate colours. Our best one was Sandpiper.

The money seemed to shrink away, but before it ran out completely people began to turn up wanting to buy our pots. We were the only pottery in the Outer Hebrides and they wanted souvenirs to take home.

'But they're awful,' we kept saying, which is a professional ceramic term for 'They're crap.'

But they still bought them.

Our two daughters sat in their playpen eating lumps of red clay while we kept practising. Fortunately we were young and enthusiastic and naive enough for it to never occur to us we might fail.

And we didn't.

I made this kitchen dresser too, and at every trade show we went to, I could have sold dozens of them.

We stuck at it and got better and kept on getting better until we were actually quite good at it and Heather ended up being able to throw sixty mugs an hour. We imported a couple from Glasgow with a mobile home who came and worked for us and no matter how many pots we made, people wanted more and we sold them all over Scotland and the top bit of England.

It was very hard work, but wonderful.

One night at 2 a.m. at the end of 18 hours' work, I saw big black beetles crawling all over the white bricks inside the kiln. There were dozens of them and they were real, except they weren't there. I was amazed that you could be so tired and not fall over. My brain knew they were a hallucination, but the beetles didn't and when I finally closed the kiln and set the controller and crawled up to bed, they were still there sitting in the dark wondering why it was getting so warm.

Even though there were quite a few more 18-hour days, I never saw the beetles again, which was a bit disappointing.

Then eventually the remoteness got too remote so we moved everything, except the couple from Glasgow who had gone native and stayed behind, to Denton Fell in the top bit of England near Hadrian's wall and a fantastic, solitary three-hundred-year-old derelict farmhouse shaped like a seven

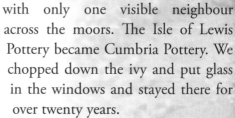

with only one visible neighbour across the moors. The Isle of Lewis Pottery became Cumbria Pottery. We chopped down the ivy and put glass in the windows and stayed there for over twenty years.

I thought I had found paradise and would never leave it until I died.

(But then in 1995 I went to the other side of the world for a week – and stayed there.)

1942 – OCTOBER 18TH

This is my mother, Kathleen Lillian Muntz, and my father, Edward Alfred Willment. From a technical point of view, this photo would have benefitted from a longer exposure, but my parents weren't together long enough for that.

They were divorced when I was too young to remember my dad. My mother then went through all her photo albums and cut out every single picture of him. So I didn't even know what he looked like until I got my grandmother's albums.

Having been brought up to believe my father was the Devil Incarnate and the nastiest child-hating creature in the universe, it was wonderful to be told by my cousin Sheila, who I met for the first time many, many years later, that my father had been a lovely man and she had adored him more than her own father – my father's only brother, Uncle George. It was so nice to hear that, but it was too late to undo all the unrelenting damage my mother had done.

1942 – I SHOULD HAVE BEEN SUSAN

My grandfather wanted a son and had three daughters. My mother and her identical twin sister were never known by their real names, but were always called 'Bill'* and 'Jim'. Their younger sister was just called Pamela.

My mother wanted a daughter, but had a son.

My Aunt Bill sent this photo of herself to my mother when she was expecting me. As you can see from the message, I should have been Susan.

It wasn't until years later I realised that people must have looked at us and thought, *What a strange family.*

But then we did have friends called Bunny and Tristram and Bertie and Torquil – names that nowadays people use for dogs and budgies, not humans – so maybe we didn't seem so strange after all.

In case you can't read it, the writing on the photo says:

To the grandest person in the world. With all my love to you and Susan. Bill.

So the message is from a woman with a man's name to her sister who is expecting a girl that turned out to be a boy.

---

* *I didn't actually find out Aunt Bill's name until I was 18 and even now I'm not sure if it was Peggy or Vivian or both.*

In later life, my mother reverted to 'Kate', but my aunt stayed Bill until she died. One of my daughters saw them walk past the window, tarted up for a night out and well past their use-by date, and said, 'Oh look, there goes Bait and Kill.'

Not perfectly identical to the trained eye. One had God. One had Gin.
See if you can tell which is which and guess which one I got.

1953 – I USED TO BE WILLMENT

My father's name was Edward Alfred Willment. So when I was born I was Colin Edward Willment, but when I was eleven my mother re-married. I'm not sure why. She proved to be a rubbish judge of character. She found my stepfather, Claude Baines Thompson, in the back of the cupboard under the stairs behind the old gasmasks and the buckets of eggs in isinglass and huge black-market tins of ham that that used to appear from time to time – food rationing didn't end in England until 1954. So Claude Baines was removed from the cupboard, dusted down, fitted with new leather patches on his elbows and became my stepfather.

I had to sign a piece of paper saying I agreed to be adopted. I was eleven, what the hell did I know and besides I was bribed with a brand new wristwatch. So I became Colin Edward Thompson.

When I was fourteen, I told myself I would change my name back when I was old enough, but I never did. Sometimes, I still wish I had.

SPOT THE DIFFERENCE

Colin Edward Willment – aged 11   Colin Edward Thompson – aged 11
(with added wristwatch)

FITTING IN – PART 23.7

I hate uniforms.

I know you need them in certain professions. You need to be able to find a policeman or a nurse when you need one. You need to know if the person trying to kill you is officially allowed to.

So why do we need them when we are little school children?

'Oh well, darling,' my mother said, 'it's so the poor children can look the same as the rest of us.'

Really mother? But, I don't think there are any poor children at my school.

We all know the truth, don't we?

School uniforms are to do exactly what they say – to make you uniform. Not to help the poor. That would be a first, wouldn't it mummy, apart from the money you put in your SPCK* missionary box each week so patronising middle-class bastards can go round the world 'rescuing' the poor ignorant savages with bibles, cigarettes, alcohol and guilt?

School uniforms are the first step on the ladder to make you fit in so you will grow up not rocking the boat.

And the poor children don't look the same as us because they haven't got posh school uniforms from Harrods like we had at boarding school. They've got clothes made out of nylon and they haven't got lovely embroidered Cash's Name Labels sewn into their anoraks have they? But then, they wouldn't be much use to them would they, because they probably can't read anyway.

'But thank you mummy for explaining everything.'

---

*   **The Society for Promoting Christian Knowledge.** *I actually had a great love for this missionary box and became quite an expert at getting money out of it with a kitchen knife. I think my mother probably never knew because she didn't empty it. She just handed it over to 'Vicar' who gave her a fresh one to fill up.*

At Ealing Grammar School for Boys, it was uniforms from day one and not just in school. If you were caught not wearing your school cap on the way to or from school on school days, the first time it was written down in a book. The second time, you were suspended for a week and the third time you were expelled. I don't remember anyone ever actually being expelled, but I did get the week's free holiday.

I had decided to go to art school when I was sixteen, which as far as Ealing Grammar School for Boys was concerned was the equivalent of becoming a professional criminal or a tramp. Had I decided to be an alcoholic or a paedophile, that would definitely have been far more acceptable.

And here are some nice Christians from our local Youth Club, trying on their Going-to-Tropical-Climes uniforms before going off to save Johnny Foreigner.

My friend Keith and I were both going to Ealing Art School and on the last day of term we took a bottle of petrol and a box of matches to school and on the green in front of the school, we made a small pile of our jackets, caps and ties, anointed them with petrol and set them on fire.

Some smaller boys cheered. Some sixth-formers said they weren't surprised and suggested we should probably kill ourselves there and then, because how could our lives go anywhere but downhill.

And then, to crown off a perfect day, a teacher came running out of the school with a fire-extinguisher and shouted at the top of his voice about how much trouble we were in.

'But, we don't go to your school any more,' we said, threw our satchels onto the fire – I took my good fountain pen out first – gave him the appropriate hand signals with both hands and ran away.

They wrote to my mother, who told me I had wasted a perfectly good jacket.

I suppose she was right. I could have given it to one of those poor children she'd been telling me about.

FRINTON-ON-SEA

Even the name sounds like a hundred years ago. I haven't been to Frinton-on-Sea since I was a little boy, I hope it hasn't changed much.

Every year my grandfather rented a house at Frinton for the summer and my mother, grandmother and I and stayed there for about six weeks. My grandfather came down at weekends. Aunts, uncles and cousins came down for occasional weeks. My cat Tigger came with us one year and showed his deep devotion to me in the way only cats can. He scratched my legs and ran away. We found him a week later, fat and content in a genteel teashop full of cream cake. He celebrated his return to the bosom of our family by scratching my legs.

The house we rented came with one of the beach huts in the photo. I think ours was the middle one because I remember the veranda had the gate in the middle. There were deckchairs and a little stove to boil the kettle and to this day if I smell burning methylated spirits it takes me right back to Frinton and the home-knitted swimming costume made of string that sagged below your knees when it got wet, which it did when the adults sent us down to the sea with our shrimping nets. There were never any shrimps. The only thing my cousins and I ever caught were colds.

Here I am in my gorgeous home-knitted swimming costume and rakish sun hat in the back garden at Frinton-on-Sea.

Rumour has it that when we went back to London, at the end of each summer, I left quite a few broken hearts behind.

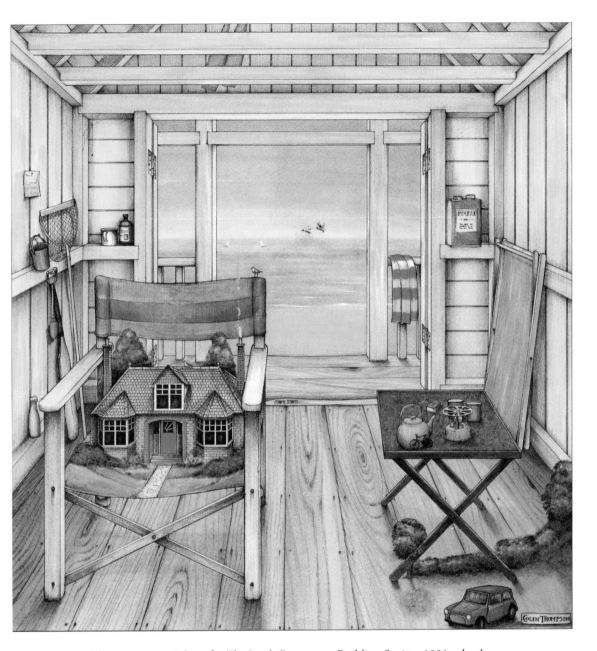

This is a picture I drew for The Leeds Permanent Building Society 1991 calendar. There in the beach hut are the shrimping net, two beach chairs and a green baize card table with the meths stove, just as I remember them from 1949. The grown-ups played a lot of cards – Bezique and Poker (but not for money – they had a jar of dried haricot beans with a metal lid you pressed in the middle to make it pop open that lived at home in Audley Road and got taken on holiday every year).

SEX EDUCATION – PART 0

Here, in the most minute detail, is all the sex education I had.

HEROES

I imagine that every child has a hero in their family. One person who seems larger than life compared to everyone else. One person who doesn't have the remoteness that most adults have.

I was lucky because I had two. One used to turn up with no announcement, be around for a few days and just as suddenly go off again – Uncle Ken, except he was my mother's cousin, so not my uncle, but my second-cousin.

'Uncle' Ken was my hero, not just because he brought me a wonderful train set from Germany or his enormous moustache, but because his whole life seemed like one huge adventure and so much more exciting than ours.

Ken was something to do with the British Forces Radio Network in Germany. I'm not sure exactly what and later he ended up travelling England as a locum, not for doctors or dentists but for pub landlords, who he then attempted to drink into bankruptcy while they were away on holiday. I'm not sure who won because in the end, he drank himself to death.

My mother always claimed Ken wanted to marry her, which I do hope wasn't true. He would have been a great dad, but I would never have wished my uptight joyless mother on him.

My other hero was my Uncle Ted. He was my real uncle, not a cousin, and married to my mother's younger sister Auntie Pamela. The rest of my family thought that Pamela had married beneath her, more than anything because Uncle Ted came from 'Up North'.

We all knew that once you travelled further than about thirty miles away from London everyone wore sacks and shoes made out of wood, especially if you went north where it was even worse. Up North, shoes were just a rumour that many people refused to believe in. It was all right to go on holiday there if you didn't stay too long and only in nice hotels, and it was even all right to buy their vegetables or bunches of violets or even possibly employ them, but one did not marry them.

Except Auntie Pamela did.

Every summer holidays Aunt Pam and Uncle Ted rescued me from my tidy quiet sterile box into a home of topsy-turvy excitement with my four cousins and an uncle who told me to pull his little finger and then farted.

A larger-than-life Uncle Ted, who rowed my cousin Stephen and me down a wide green Shropshire river and told us that if we touched any of the brass screws in the bottom of the boat it would fall apart and sink.

So we sat clutching our knees trying to hold our feet in the air because the water looked so cold and neither of us could swim.

Giant Uncle Ted, who at weekends took us into the empty laundry where he was the manager and let us ride the conveyor belts up into the roof, high over the silent machines, and fall off the end onto mountains of dirty clothes.

Mad Uncle Ted, who one afternoon played William Tell with the dartboard on the back of the kitchen door and missed and threw a dart into the top of my cousin Stephen's head as he stood stock-still beneath it.

Spellbinding Uncle Ted, who drove down Scottish country lanes in his laundry van with Stephen on his lap holding the steering wheel and me sitting high up behind them on brown paper parcels of washing, and when Stephen crashed the van into a narrow stone bridge, just burst out laughing and didn't stop laughing until we got back to the house in Dumfries, where one night the kitchen ceiling fell down and rats ran across the beds in the darkness, even though there were nine cats in the house, including one which Stephen's little sister Christine dressed up in her doll's clothes and put to bed in her doll's pram, and another cat, a genuine Scottish Wildcat – or so Uncle Ted said when it sank its teeth into his thumb.

My wonderful uncle, who made the empty space in my heart where my father should have been feel emptier than ever and yet filled it up with light and laughter.

My wonderful, wonderful uncle, so different from my remote grandfather and the rest of my family, who I wished so much was my father, an uncle that I loved like no one else, an uncle that everyone should have one like.

Life with Pam and Ted was one long adventure and I never wanted to go home. It was like being deliriously happy drunk and the sombre silence of my own home was the hangover, stone cold sober and full of sadness.

Life with Auntie Pam and Uncle Ted was how life should be and I lived from one school holiday to the next holding on to tiny details that other people with normal lives forgot because they could take them for granted.

When I was with them, it felt as if my eyes were wide open all the time, and that back at home I was half-asleep, part of me switched off.

Stephen and I would lie in bed at night and talk until we fell asleep. Sometimes we didn't clean our teeth. Sometimes we didn't wash our faces and we never knelt by our beds with our hands clasped to say our prayers.

If Auntie Pam had had her way, I would never have gone home, just moved in and lived with them as their fifth child. My loving mother even agreed at one point to Pam and Ted adopting me, but my grandmother put a stop to that because of what the neighbours might think.

Every year they seemed to live somewhere different, places that were far away and exotic – Shropshire, Dumfries, Cornwall. I think Uncle Ted got restless, maybe they all did, because they never seemed to stay in one place for long.

Not like us. We had our feet nailed to the ground. Everyone in Audley Road, Ealing, London, W5 did. I was born in the Old Court Nursing Home round the corner, baptised and went to Sunday School in the church round another corner, and went to school down the road.

We were all like that round there, because we knew our place and we knew it didn't get any better than that.

But Uncle Ted had a head full of dreams – nothing dramatic like moving to Australia, but where his dreams flew his body and his family followed. Their homes were always full of half-unpacked cardboard boxes as if they never knew when the wanderlust might take them again, so there was no point in unwrapping everything, just what they needed there and then.

The boxes with their newspaper nests were always home to a troupe of cats that travelled the country with them, stragglers left behind here, new kittens adopted there.

Every summer I spent the holidays somewhere new, in places that were full of excitement, places that to most people were probably quite ordinary, but places where life might suddenly break out of its rigid repetition and burst into song.

Cornwall was the best. I was fifteen by then, but life with Pam and Ted was still a wonderful adventure of illicit happiness. And when I look back, I realised they just lived a normal life that thousands of families everywhere did and none of it was illicit at all.

Normal people often left the washing-up until the next morning and didn't get into trouble or feel guilty about it. Normal people told dirty jokes and laughed unashamedly at them and sometimes went to bed in their vests. They didn't kneel on the floor every night, hands clasped, eyes uplifted to some invisible fiction, asking for blessings and forgiveness from some demanding spirit that lived above the ceiling and could never be satisfied.

Normal people gloried in the simple joys of life, sitting in the sun, drinking beer, playing football with their kids, leaving the dust to gather on top of the wardrobes. Life rough around the edges, frayed carpets, frayed tempers sometimes, running indoors, lying on the bed with their shoes on, digging holes in the garden – I wanted that.

Most of the photos in this book are from my grandmother's and my mother's photograph albums. It says a lot about my family's self-importance that the ONLY photos with my Uncle Ted in are four pictures from their wedding in 1944. There are dozens and dozens of photos from many years of my Aunt Bill's husband Guy – the one who use to take his belt to my cousin Jenny if she wet the bed, but then my Aunt Bill must have told him otherwise he wouldn't have known. But then, Uncle Guy came from our side of the tracks. So that was OK.

STYLE – I HAS IT

I was at the cutting edge of fashion right from the very start, as you can see.

The photo says it all: 'Colin in first long trousers.' I was almost thirteen and the last one in my class to stop going to school in shorts. Most of the other boys had got into long trousers by the time they were ten. I imagine the reason was because shorts were probably two shillings cheaper.

Photographs were a sort of grey-brown colour when I was a little boy. So I've added the yellow to my Mac and Souwester to show you just how fashionable I was and highlighted my wonderful Red Leather Gaiters, which had the girls in Savernake Kindergarten falling at my feet.Is it any wonder I grew up colour blind?

Looks can be deceiving. I promise you I was NEVER a hippy. I'm far too cynical. I was simply scruffy.

OH GOD

It's not the photo of
me saying my prayers
that is so terrible,
it's the fact that my
mother actually
wanted to record it.

There were parts of growing up when it wasn't just the photographs that
were out of focus.

I actually had a soprano voice like an angel and passed the audition to
go to Westminster Choir School – but my voice and faith broke at about the
same time.

1948, 1949, 1950, 1951, 1952, 1953 – HOW TO COMPLETELY FUCK UP YOUR ONLY CHILD FOREVER WITH ONE SIMPLE SENTENCE

'Where's my daddy?'

'He was a horrid fat man who didn't like children so I sent him away.'

This fiction was repeated every time I asked the question and I was sixteen before I discovered the truth.

He fucked someone else.

No, he was a horrid fat man who didn't like children so he got sent away, which, of course, meant it was all my fault.

My mother then married God, but there was no Baby Jesus to be my brother.

1950 – MY BEST FRIEND

This is a photo of me and my best friend Tigger. I had a black cat before this, but I can't remember his name. I do remember that he gave me ringworm, which I was never told was not actually a worm, so was quite frightening. I had to go to hospital and have an ultraviolet light shone on my hair and then I think they put ointment on me and pulled some hairs out. I don't know how often this happened, but it was more than once.

As for the cat, they killed him.

Then Tigger arrived and was my best friend until I was sent to boarding school.

While I was away at school, they killed him too, but told me he pined away because I wasn't there, which meant it was my fault.* He was three years old. It was many years before I realised that cats are far too selfish to pine away.

When I was fourteen I built a big cage in my parent's flat and got eight budgies and each one was a different colour.

While I was on holiday in Cornwall at Aunt Pam's, my stepfather gave them and their cage away to an old people's home.

---

*   *I think a pattern of guilt was emerging here.*

1949 – MUMMIES AND DADDIES

'Why do I always have to be the mummy?' Anna, the girl next door, asked. 'Because you're the girl,' I told her.

'I want to be the daddy,' she said.

'Well, I'm the daddy. You have to be the mummy and stay at home with the baby and cook the dinner.'

We were both seven years old. Her mummy and daddy came from Greece and we were standing in the gloom of the abandoned air-raid shelter in their back garden.

Every house down Audley Road built a shelter during the war. Some were no more than corrugated tin covered with earth. They had been taken down years ago. Others, built of concrete, had been harder to demolish and a lot of people had just covered them with climbing roses and kept the lawnmower in there.

My grandparents had built their shelter underground in the front garden. As a baby, I slept through long nights in it, safe in the comforting smells of damp earth and condensed milk. A few miles away London had burned, but out in the suburbs the nights were generally calm and uneventful. Only one house in our street had been hit by a bomb. Our shelter had been sealed up and hidden under crazy paving and a bed of rose bushes, a tomb of ghosts and darkness. I imagine it's still down there and whoever owns the house now won't have the faintest idea it's there.

I was born during the war, but I was only three when it ended and I have no memories of it, but its remnants and aftermath were still around. As my grandfather drove me through London in our big blue Wolseley, I peered over the edge of the window at a different world, a post-war gloom where grey kids with dirty faces and toy swords played on exciting-looking bomb sites in streets where the houses had no gardens or bathrooms. There was nothing like that in Ealing, W5. You could hear a pin drop three streets away. Our world was laid out in tidy squares, clean suburbs, nice gardens. I had an electric train set Uncle Ken brought me from Germany and a big wooden fort my grandfather got made by a German prisoner of war, with a place in the bottom where I could keep all my soldiers and tanks.

We didn't just live on the right side of the tracks, we owned the factories that made the tracks and the trains that ran on them. Except we didn't personally. My family actually owned the factories that had made the surgical

instruments to mend our wounded soldiers. The war, that killed so many, made my family rich.

'Well, I want to be the daddy,' Anna said. 'It's my house so I can say.'

'Oh, all right then.'

'Well, I'm off to work now,' Anna said, 'and when I come home you can have a baby.'

'All right.'

I poured some water out of a jam jar into tin of earth and stirred it round and round with an old spoon.

'I'll get the dinner ready,' I said.

'OK,' Anna said and walked off down the garden towards the blackcurrant bushes. I sat in the darkness of the air-raid shelter, stirring the mud. I stood up and rocked Anna's doll's pram backwards and forwards like I'd seen her do. The doll looked up at me with one eye shut and the other stuck wide open.

I could see cobwebs on the ceiling and thought of all the spiders hanging in the shadows looking down at me. They were all going to fall down the back of my neck and drop their cobwebs on my face.

My mother screamed at spiders and taught me to.

I dropped the spoon and ran out into the sunshine.

'The baby's crying,' I told Anna, who was sitting on the grass stroking my cat Tigger.

'Well, you're the mummy,' she said. 'It probably wants its nappy changed.'

'I think it wants to come out into the garden,' I said.

'It can't,' said Anna. 'It's got to have a sleep.'

'I don't want to play any more.'

'But I haven't come home from work yet,' Anna said.

'Well, I don't like being the mummy,' I replied. 'I want to go home.'

'I'll show you my wee-wee,' Anna said.

'I've seen it,' I said. 'You haven't got one.'

Tigger wandered off across the lawn and jumped back over the fence into my garden and I went home after him.

A MOTHER'S WIT AND WISDOM*
*There was actually NO wit and very little wisdom

Putting her pen down on the desk – *'Now you, stay there.'*
This was said in such a way that the pen was always too scared to move.

SIBLINGS

I always assumed that my father had married again, and he had. I also assumed that he and his new wife undoubtedly had children so somewhere in the world I had half-brothers and sisters.

I even dreamt he might turn up one day and say, *'Hello, I'm your father and these are your brothers and sisters.'* But it never happened.

Or maybe I would meet someone and we'd chat and then discover we were brother and sister. That never happened either. Yet I was convinced into my mid-forties that I had to have siblings. The odds were strongly for it.

I only met my father once. I was nineteen and just married to Sue and thought I should find him. It was quite difficult, but eventually I tracked him down. It was bad for both of us. We were total strangers and felt so awkward with each other that we never met again. By the time I thought of trying again, I had moved hundreds of miles away.

And then one day, I was standing in the kitchen at Denton Fell and my wife Heather said, 'Oh by the way, your dad's dead. I forgot to tell you.' He was sixty-five.

And that was it. Everyone said he never had any more children, but there is still a little part of me that thinks they're lying to me. It would be so amazing and wonderful.

DON'T BE SUCH A BABY

When you're a child everything is stories. Stories and the real world are all the same because you question nothing.

Adults were there to make your decisions. Peter Pan was as real as electricity. God was as real as my cat Tigger and, if you were lucky, as you grew up, you sorted out truth from fiction.

As I grew up I realised that most of what I had been told was fiction.

Tigger was real because he scratched me. God, Father Christmas, Alice in Wonderland, my mother telling me how much she loved me, and even my father were all lies, because that's what fiction is – a polite word for telling lies. The more I looked, the more lies I found and the more I moved into a solitary world of my own.

And being true didn't always make things right. Even half the stuff that was true was rubbish, designed to put me in a box with all the other boxes, crammed into the darkness of a railway truck on an endless Möbius strip rattling away for eternity. In the end you have to decide on your own truths, but at eleven the lies just leave a vacuum. To a child, the world is a village. The scale of place means as far as you can see, and all the rest is pictures. There are no connections, just the small horizon of a small person.

My bed was an island in this world, my kingdom of escape and dreams, a bed so wide and me so small that when I lay on my back and stretched my arms out I couldn't touch both sides. When I stood on the floor, the sheets were level with my waist and I had to pull myself up to climb into bed. But instead of feeling lost in this giant's bed, I felt safe and secure. It was my world alone, no one else's, a ship in a sea of darkness. I could sink into the feather pillows, stretch out under the fresh cotton sheets and float away into a silent world of dreams.

The house was always quiet, no radio, no music and almost no television. If a cat coughed two streets away, we all knew about it. For one hour each afternoon the doors of the old television cabinet were opened and I sat cross-legged on the lounge floor, alone in the room, and watched the children's programmes on the small grey screen. Refined ladies from the best schools talked down to jerky marionettes made out of flowerpots and naughty glove puppets to entertain the few of us rich enough and therefore nice enough to own a television.

Boundaries were reinforced from afar. The cotton wool was packed around me. I was safe and sterilised and everything was in balance. In the kitchen my mother and grandmother made dinner while my grandfather drove home from work. Sometimes the door moved and Tigger came in smelling of Kit-e-kat and rubbed around my legs. The television was older than me, the pictures blurred and colourless, but it was a window into another world, a world where order was sometimes not as well balanced as my world, a world I never visited. When Elizabeth II was crowned queen in 1953, my mother took photographs of the TV screen with her Brownie box camera.

My grandfather had bought the TV in 1939 and for the five years of war it had stood locked shut in the corner gathering dust until 1945 when programmes started up again. My grandmother dusted it off, opened the doors and life resumed, almost in mid-sentence, as if nothing had happened.

At six o'clock every night we sat in the dining room and ate dinner. We bowed our heads and thanked God for what we were about to receive. It was a little ritual of my mother's. The rest of us sat through it staring into our napkins. If we should have been thanking anyone, it should have been Papa who made the money to buy the food and Nana who had cooked it.

After dinner God went back to what he'd been doing before we'd asked him to bless our meat and two veg. Papa drank whisky and dozed while the women did the washing-up. The clock ticked on the mantelpiece. It chimed on the hour. War had faded into the past and all was well in the world.

I went back up to my room and sat on my wonderful bed. Tigger was already there, curled up, purring softly to himself. He opened his eyes and stared at me, and then went back to sleep while I hid in a book or drew pictures, unless it was Friday, which was bath night – hot water with Dettol, which my grandfather got in gallon cans, filled the water with white clouds.

Whatever was the matter with me – measles (British and German versions), mumps, whooping cough, scarlet fever or the flu (I worked my way through all of them) – my mother made me drink orange juice, glasses and glasses of it to wash the germs out of my body.

Apparently germs were terrified of orange juice.

I enjoyed being ill, not seriously ill, just unwell enough for my grandmother to say I looked poorly and stop my mother sending me to school.

For several years I had the perfect childhood illness. As far as anyone ever discovered, there was nothing at all wrong with me except my temperature was a degree and a half higher than it was supposed to be. It was brilliant. I was taken to all sorts of specialists and had all sorts of tests and was diagnosed with *There's absolutely nothing at all wrong with him except his temperature is one and a half degrees higher than it should be Syndrome.*

It was enough to keep me off school for days or even weeks every time I told Nana I didn't feel well. My mother feebly protested that I was fine, but Nana was in charge and her word was law.

It wasn't that I didn't like school, I did. I was a good boy and always near the top of the class, always well behaved and showered with praise. It was just that being on my own at home in bed was better. I could lie in bed surrounded by my favourite toys and spend the whole day away in my land of daydreams. Sparrows chattered outside the window, pigeons sat in the gutter and talked softly to each other. Downstairs I could hear the murmur of my grandmother and mother talking in the kitchen. The milkman would come rattling glass bottles at the front door and four houses away their dog barked at him.

Theoretically ill and half-asleep in a twilight world between day and night, safe in my bed, I could let the sounds of the world drift through my head while I sailed away to places where there was no loneliness. Nana used to brings me biscuits and sweets and let Tigger back in.

But the days in bed didn't come entirely without a price. Doctor Vinter, with his thick German accent, was called. He would take my temperature and hold my thin wrist in his great red hands to feel my pulse. Then I'd have to sit

up and lift my pyjama jacket and vest and say 'ninety-nine' while he tapped my chest and listened to my breathing. And that was all fine until we got to the bit I dreaded. As soon as the doctor said 'open wide', I felt myself beginning to heave, and the tight grip of dizzy fear, like my nightmares, clutched my throat and starved my breath. It was the same every time, I was going to suffocate to death and no one seemed to care.

'Don't be such a baby,' my mother would snap as the doctor pushed a flat stick the size of a cricket bat into my mouth and told me to say 'aaahhh'.

I was about to choke to death.

I knew I was.

I could feel my whole life tied up in a terrifying knot that was suffocating me while mother kept telling me not to be a baby.

The doctor decided I was a sickly child and left a bottle of chloromycetin tablets.

My mother ushered the old man out of the room with reverent gestures, reserved for doctors and vicars, while I hurried back into my dreams as quickly as I could.

Every four months there were trips to the dentist for 'a checkup'. This was worse than the doctor. My mother took me to a large Victorian house on Ealing Common, large still rooms with tall ceilings and potted plants, large chairs and a large man with large hands who lifted me into a large chair in a large room where the air stood perfectly still. The drill was like a twisted reject from a Frankenstein movie, a tangle of peeling chrome pulley wheels and cables racing round as the rasping bit bored into my teeth like a tiny road drill. There were no injections to kill the pain in those days.

My mother sat at the back of the room and said, 'Don't be such a baby.'

Thank you, Mummy. I feel better now, happy in the knowledge that Baby Jesus is looking down on me and will keep me safe.

First there was the painless bit, a loud noise that went right through me, shaking every part of my body. Then there was the fire, scalding pain that seemed as if it would never end, sharp cutting lines that went right through every nerve.

'There we are,' says the dentist. 'That wasn't so bad, was it?'

And I always shook my head, too scared to be thought a baby, fighting back the tears and just relieved it was over. This went gone on for years, long into the days when I was old enough to make my own choices and painkilling

injections were available because there was always this voice in my head telling me only babies and girls had injections.

I think pain brought my mother closer to her God. For me, it just convinced me more and more that he didn't exist. There were visits with no fillings and then there were visits where teeth were pulled out. And that was the worst of all, with the man in the black suit holding the gas mask over my face while I fought to stay alive. That is a terror you never forget. There was the pain afterwards too and a mouthful of blood and nothing to make it better because my mother didn't believe children should take aspirins.

'Don't be such a baby,' she would say. 'They were only baby teeth.'

I was also six when they took my tonsils out. Once again, I fought the gasmask as the terror of death overtook me. This time my mother wasn't there with her helpful advice. I'd been wheeled away into the operating theatre but she was sitting by my bed when I was back in a ward full of grown-up men because there were no spare beds in the children's ward. I couldn't stop coughing – the stitches in my throat came undone and I coughed blood.

'Don't be such a baby,' she said. 'It's only a little bit of blood.'

But I was six, I only had a little bit.

This was the British way, remote and cold with a stiff upper lip that built your character. No good could ever come from showing your feelings or taking pain medication. That was the sort of thing foreigners did.

In 1999 I finally succeeded in building a time machine.

1952 – SEX EDUCATION – PART 1

Forest Hall* Boarding School – Yorkshire – I'm
third from the left looking at my feet.

There were more than a hundred acres of thick North Yorkshire woods, and in front of them at the top of a hill was the school, a beautiful country mansion like something out of a children's story.

Sixty boys and ten staff. It looked like paradise, but it was a prison, too far from anywhere to run away from, though one boy did and was found drowned in the river a few days later. It looked like a childhood dream, long days of Latin and cricket, of playing in the trees, cross-country running and training to become a leader of men, uniforms and views of the world from Harrods, privilege for the privileged in yet another isolated cocoon. But there was a darkness about the place like an invisible cloak, a darkness that could stifle innocence, a darkness like a memory of Charles Dickens.

---

* Forest Hall *is now a very smart hotel and spa. I wonder if they'd give me a discount.*

43

There were six of us in the woods behind the school. Past the outbuildings and the copse where the pheasants were fed, across the field where the goats grew fat on damp grass, the woods were thick with old oak trees and rumours of a secret tunnel leading back to the cellars below the school, where big boys took new boys, blindfolded and shaking with fear, and made them eat live worms. The worms were tinned spaghetti, but a terrified child has a terrified imagination and most of us believed that what we were eating was alive and more than one boy threw up down his shirt and was punished by matron.

Bluebells were growing in the lakes of sunshine between the trees. The air was warm with spring softness and on the bank behind us the primroses were coming out. Pigeons were whispering softly in the treetops, unaware that the children below them would be blasting them to death with shotguns in a few weeks' time.

Badgers, foxes and squirrels were spring-cleaning. The sap was rising everywhere, even in us unsuspecting ten-year-olds.

'Can you make yours go hard?' Smith One said.

'Of course I can,' I said. 'Everybody can. Can't they?'

'Girls can't,' Huntly-Jones said and we all giggled.

'Girls haven't got one,' I said.

'Do you know why?' said Porter.

'Er, no,' I said. 'They just haven't.'

'It's to make babies,' said Porter.

'What do you mean?' Huntly-Jones asked.

'My brother told me,' Porter explained. 'You put your thing inside their hole and they have a baby.'

'Don't be stupid.'

'That's why it gets hard,' said Huntly-Jones. 'So you can push it inside them.'

'That's disgusting.'

'In where?' I asked.

'They've got a hole,' Huntly-Jones told us.

'Don't be stupid,' I said, 'that's where they wee-wee.'

'No, they've got another one,' Huntly-Jones said.

'That's where they poo-poo,' Jenkins sniggered, and we all giggled again.

'I'm not pushing my thingy in a girl's bottom.'

This remark was prophetically ironic because some years later Jenkins was arrested in London for trying to push his thingy inside a young man's bottom.

44

'No, it's a special hole for babies,' Huntly-Jones informed us.

We all stood in silence for a bit. Jenkins undid his fly-buttons and began playing with himself and one by one so did the rest of us.

'Yours isn't very big,' I said, looking at Jenkins, 'and it's all funny at the end.'

Jenkins was the only boy who hadn't been circumcised. He rolled back his foreskin and waved his tiny penis at everyone. It looked horrible.

'That's because you've all had the ends cut off yours,' he said.

'Don't be stupid,' said Smith Two.

'What would they do that for?'

'Dunno,' said Jenkins, 'but it's true.'

'This stuff with making babies,' Harcourt asked. 'Are you sure?'

'Yes, my brother showed me a book,' Porter said, 'with drawings. The woman lies down and the man lies on top of her and puts his thing inside her and she has a baby.'

'That's stupid,' said Jenkins. 'My mummy and daddy wouldn't do that, it's dirty.'

'It's true,' said Huntly-Jones.

'My mummy and daddy wouldn't,' Jenkins insisted.

'They did,' Huntly-Jones laughed. 'That's how they got you.'

'It's called sexualintercourse,' said Porter.

'Your parents did sexualintercourse,' said Huntly-Jones.

'I'll bash you if you say that again,' Jenkins said and started crying.

The rest of us stood in a circle pulling at ourselves. Jenkins said he was going to tell matron what we'd said, but we said if he did we'd put him out on the top window ledge and cut the end off his penis too.

'And I'll tell her you touched mine in the showers,' I said.

'And mine,' said Porter.

'And mine,' said Huntly-Jones.

'He's touched everybody's,' Harcourt said, which was true.

Jenkins had even touched the headmaster's but then so had quite a few boys, but it was all right because he'd touched ours. Mr Harris, the headmaster, who actually owned Forest Hall, liked touching our willies.

He didn't touch everyone's, just the nice-looking boys.

'My Pretty Angels,' he called us.

I thought it might be naughty, but I wasn't sure why and beside no one said anything, not even the teachers, and they must have known about it, so

I guessed it was all right. In the evening about six of us went to his bedroom for 'extra lessons' and we all took our clothes off and stood in a circle while Mr Harris stroked us. He took his clothes off too and played with himself. Sometimes he knelt down and sucked our willies. I liked that, because it got hard and felt really nice.

One day I was in his room and while he was sucking me, he put his finger up my bottom.

'Can I put my willie there?' he asked, but I shook my head.

He asked me if I would like to suck him. I didn't want to. He had a really tiny willie. It was smaller than mine, but I was a bit frightened to touch it. He put his arms round me and pressed his willie up against mine and held them both in his hand at the same time. Then he started groaning and then this funny white stuff came out of his willie all over my tummy.

He said if I would suck him, he'd make me a prefect. So I did. It tasted salty and after a bit, he pulled it out of my mouth and more white stuff came out. When I told the others in the dorm, Huntly-Jones said that was the stuff you put inside a lady to make babies.

'It's called sperms,' he told us.

Mr Harris said he'd take me to Switzerland in the holidays with some other boys, like he did every year, but my mother wouldn't let me go.

That's how I learnt the facts of life, standing in a circle with the sons of the wealthy, wanking in an old oak forest in the Yorkshire hills. I found it very difficult to imagine grown-ups taking off their clothes and doing it, especially my mother and grandparents, but I knew it was true and it sounded quite exciting and I wanted to do it.

FEBRUARY 6TH 1952

I was ill in bed, under the sheets making tunnels with books. Tigger was under the covers down at my feet staring up at me as I pushed toy cars down the tunnels.

'The King's bed,' a muffled voice over by the door said and I came up to find my mother sitting on the eiderdown.

'What?'

'The King's dead,' my mother repeated.

'Oh, I thought you said the King's bed,' I said and went back to my tunnels.

'Is that Tigger down there?' my mother said.

'Yes.'

'Well, get him out. I've told you about having the cat in the bed.'

'But he likes it,' I said, and so did I.

She didn't like the cat being in the room. She didn't like the affection he showed me or the affection I showed him, affection she couldn't evoke or match. I used to hide Tigger in the bed in the evening and if I got away with it, my mother would have to get up in the middle of the night and let him out into the garden. No one seemed to notice that when Tigger was there I never had nightmares or wet the bed.

1954 – SEX EDUCATION – PART 2

You have to be older than twelve to fuck.

When I was twelve I went to stay with my cousins in the summer holidays and one afternoon, left alone in the house with my eleven-year-old cousin Jenny, we tried to do sexualintercoursing. We took all our clothes off and Jenny lay on the edge of the bed with her legs open and I got stiff. She'd never seen it like that before and was fascinated. I told her about sexualintercoursing and that was why I'd gone hard, so I could put it inside her.

'Do you want to do it?' I asked.

'Yes,' she said.

So I stood in front of her at the end of the bed and pushed.

'Ow,' she said.

'You're supposed to have a hole where babies come out,' I said. 'Where is it?'

'I don't know,' she said.

'Maybe you're not old enough,' I said. 'Maybe you don't get the hole for babies until you're grown up.'

I knelt on the floor and had a look, but I couldn't see any holes, just little wet pink bits, so I sat on the bed and rubbed myself for a bit while she and my aunt's old dog sat and watched until I got the feeling. I was getting a few drops of white stuff by then and it tasted salty. Jenny and I tasted it and made the dog taste it too. She wagged her tail but I don't think she liked it any more than we did. Then we went out and played in the garden until Aunt Bill came home at tea time.

MY BEST FRIEND – MIKE DIMARCO

Mike is my oldest friend. We were at school together. No, we are NOT holding hands. And by the way, EVERYONE stood like that in the sixties. And that is my daughter Charlotte showing a flower to her mother Sue, who was taking the photo. We were all pretending not to notice that Mike was wearing a cardigan.

1958 – TRANSPORT

My first motorbike was one of these – a 1947 125cc Royal Enfield with a gear lever on the petrol tank. It had died and probably been buried a few years before I got it because it broke down all the time. My girlfriends hated it because with two people on it, it was slower than walking and they were always complaining about getting engine oil on their clothes. In the end I had to sell it to pay for its repairs when it broke down in Brighton.

My second and third motorbikes were little better – tired old 125cc BSA Bantams that the Post Office had worn out delivering telegrams. All my early motorbikes had two things in common – they were cheap and unreliable. But then, I suppose I was too.

SEX & DRUGS & ROCK-N-ROLL

In the sixties we were all supposed to have as much sex and drugs and rock and roll as possible.

Sex was my favourite. It was free – as long as you overlooked the potential consequences – and, most of the time, absolutely fantastic.

Rock and roll was fantastic too because we had invented it, the same as sex. Our parents had listened to music by people who wore suits and had tidy haircuts like they did and played in dance bands. And, of course, our parents never had sex more than the one time it had taken to produce us and it had always been with the light out, eyes shut tight, thinking of England as they did their duty while wearing thick pyjamas.

Drugs were something I was much too scared to try. I loved myself too much to take anything that could be dangerous. Not that there was much choice in the sixties. It was mainly pot, which I found pretty boring. It didn't so much enhance life as send it to sleep. The other new toy was LSD and there was no way I was ever going to try that, not with the thousands of people we kept hearing about who suddenly thought they were birds and flew off the tops of tall buildings. At least two people I knew were changed forever by it.

Drink was a different matter altogether. Well, it was for a while, until I finally connected the throwing up and feeling really shit for hours after about five minutes of feeling great with the cheap cider I was drinking. I finally realised I had almost no head for alcohol and thank goodness I didn't because I would probably have become an alcoholic.

Smoking – I did have a head for that and from sixteen to thirty-five I chain-smoked all day every day. Twenty-five years later, when I was fifty-nine, smoking was blamed when I had bypass surgery for a blocked artery.

MUSIC MUSIC MUSIC

To understand how important The Ealing Club was, you have to understand how important Ealing wasn't. We used to say that if there were elephants in England, Ealing is where they would have gone to die.

And they did. Ealing was the graveyard where lots of the old soldiers who had shot elephants and the natives in India retired to die. They kept their dying to themselves and did it very quietly with occasional visits to the saloon bar for a snifter of port and afternoon tea at The House of Tong.

In streets of big Victorian houses, old colonels, retired from a life of subjugating the world, sat behind yellowing lace curtains in gloomy rooms that had remained unchanged since they were children, except that as time passed, cigarette smoke had made everything even darker, even their dreams.

They were forgotten but not gone. The stag at bay, once standing in the afternoon sun, now hid behind the faded varnish of evening. In our west London suburb, there were endless streets of these quiet Victorian houses with their quiet Victorian owners dying off one by one. They had travelled the globe taking their civilisation to poor underprivileged Johnny Foreigner and then retired to Ealing to sit in the twilight, the blood washed from their hands and consciences, waiting for God to call them to paradise where everyone would be white and know their place and three rooms away you could always hear a song by Vera Lynn.

Ealing was also a memory of movies where even the villains spoke like toffs. Alec Guinness in black and white, genteel, finely crafted entertainment with added *Carry-On* films. I went to school next door to Ealing Studios

and stared at Anita Ekberg's disturbing chest as she and Anthony Steele were whisked away to the country for the weekend.

As I moved through my childhood and teenage bits, Ealing began to change. As the old soldiers died one by one, their houses were converted into flats and bedsitters. But it was still genteel and quiet.

We knew our place.

It was middle-class veering slightly towards upper-middle-class with a desperate desire to be upper-upper-middle-class, and maybe even drop the 'middle'. We had accounts at the grocer's and a little woman my grandmother called 'the daily' who came in and did twice a week. My mother and aunts were brought up by nannies who wore uniforms and pushed their prams around Ealing Common in a convoy with an accuracy you could set your watch by. We had a button in every room that rang a bell in the kitchen.

We were very sure of our place. No man may be an island but a suburb certainly could be. Ealing had a moat around it to keep it safe from West Ealing, South Ealing and all the other common places beyond. Our blood was blue, which was strange because our necks were red.

Yet, no one would have had it any other way.

Familiarity breeds contentment.

Each morning, the milk floats radiated out from United Dairies on the edge of the Common. The horses I remember as child were replaced by the hum of electric motors as the floats stopped and started, stopped and started along our peaceful streets.

The price of all this security was a wet blanket that lay over Ealing, smothering laughter, dampening down rash decisions, muffling raised voices, but it kept us safe and warm.

As I grew up, the only music I heard in our house were ancient 78s of Caruso singing opera which my mother adored. Like her, it was cold and mechanical, an overbearing photocopy of real feelings – not from the heart, but from an inflexible book of rules.

But then, in the mid-fifties, we discovered Eel Pie Island. We'd take the bus or go on our motorbikes out to Twickenham where the enchanted island sat in the Thames.

We'd cross the footbridge with an old lady in a cupboard at the far end that you gave sixpence to and enter another world. And it was enchanted,

with a small group of eccentric cottages of artists and inventors – including Trevor Baylis, who created the clockwork radio.

Beyond the cottages was the Eel Pie Island Hotel, which always looked like it was just about to start falling down. It had a wonderful ballroom with a sprung floor and every now and then, when everyone managed to dance up and down at the same time, it was like standing up drunk on a gigantic water bed.

And there, helped by cheap cider, I learnt to jive as Chris Barber played trad jazz until it felt as if all the air in the ballroom had been used up and we collapsed in the grass outside and watched the River Thames sail serenely by.

This wasn't opera. The words could have been any words. It wasn't what they said, but how they said it. And every note pressed buttons that made it impossible to sit still. It was like all the walls of my home had fallen down around me and the other houses had vanished and the trees and the shops and the cars and everything that had always been in the way had gone too, and now I could see, for the first time in my life, that if there was a horizon in the world, it was so far away that it might as well have not be there.

It poured colour over the grey world of post-war England, garish lurid fairground sparkle glitter paint that no amount of repression and criticism could wash away. It changed the world, and when Chuck Berry sang 'Sweet Little Sixteen', it was better than sex. At least, it was until I actually had sex.

At eleven o'clock we'd all stagger back over the bridge from the island into the real world and someone would say, 'Let's go down to Brighton.'

So we did.

We hitchhiked at midnight or scrounged a lift or drove our motorbikes the sixty-five or so miles down to the cold stony beach and all huddled together telling ourselves what a great time we were having, because we were rebel beatniks refusing to follow the rules, at least until we went back to school or work at nine o'clock sharp on Monday morning.

By the time we arrived in Brighton everything was closed and had gone to bed so we all tried to sleep, but it was usually too cold and when the grey daylight arrived, everything was still closed and in bed so we hitchhiked back to London or got cheap rides on the milk-train or kicked and swore at our motorbikes which were also closed and asleep.

And the wonderful ridiculous thing was that lots of us did it all over again the next weekend.

Jazz gave way to rock and roll and rhythm and blues and then in March 1962, only five minutes' walk from where I lived, The Ealing Club arrived – the thin end of the wedge that would change the world forever. Standards were falling. There would be tears before bed time and even Baby Jesus would not be able to save us.

Between two shops by the railway, a set of stone steps led down into the darkness to a footpath that followed the railway for a few hundred yards before turning left into a lane of narrow workshops and coming out again at the shops around the corner, and at the bottom of the steps was The Ealing Club, which was started by a Scotsman in tartan trousers called Alexis Korner.

It was another world, something far too alien to have come from another country, but something that must have travelled across galaxies. For a start there was noise, not accidental noise, but magnificent noise that carried a hypnotic beat. Someone had picked up a piece of New Orleans, magnified it and dropped it in Ealing, where it shouted so loud it drowned out any protests.

The first time I heard it, I was hooked. The music leapt into my veins and burst into my head with frantic excitement. Rhythm and blues synchronised with the beat of my heart, a door opened that would never close and I flew to another world.

The man on the stage with the guitar had skin-tight tartan trousers and pointed shoes and wild hair, and magic came out of his mouth. Alexis Korner sang the blues, and over the next eternity there were more guitars and there was more noise. And not just any noise, but noise that was the beginning of greatness.

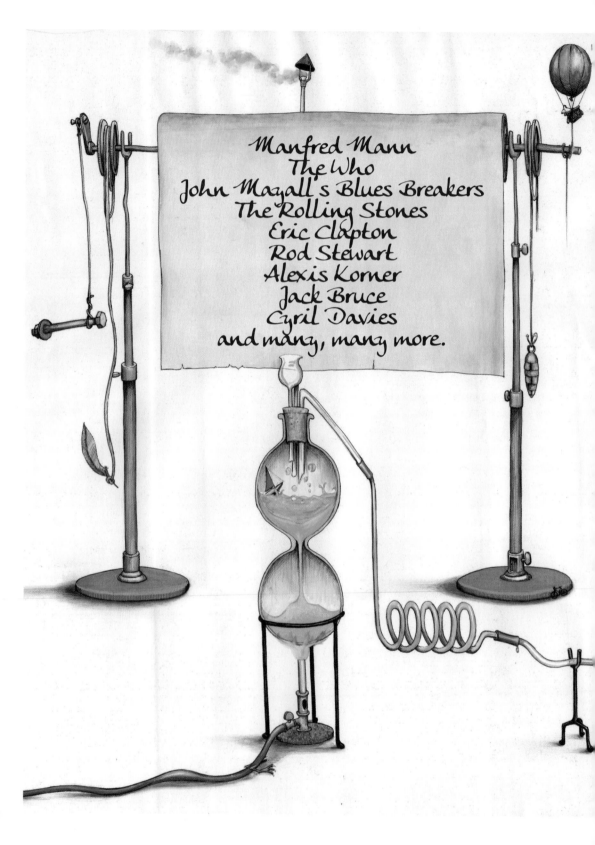

Manfred Mann
The Who
John Mayall's Blues Breakers
The Rolling Stones
Eric Clapton
Rod Stewart
Alexis Korner
Jack Bruce
Cyril Davies
and many, many more.

Then everything changed.

On January 13th 1963, I saw a play on TV, which the BBC have managed to destroy every single copy of. It was called *The Madhouse on Castle Street* and Bob Dylan spent the time sitting on the stairs playing the guitar and singing.

And very soon after that his first album came out, and bits of me that had been asleep woke up and stayed awake forever.

And it did matter what those words were.

They came from another world too and even when they didn't make sense they said everything.

I didn't want to dance around the room.

I didn't even want to stand up.

I didn't know why, but I knew that things would never be the same again. And a massive, wonderful sadness woke up inside me and everything seemed to get bigger and bigger.

I saw him play at the Festival Hall, young, nervous, alone and tiny in the middle of a massive stage, and again at the Albert Hall with a group and much later at Earls Court after which he lost his magic and got polluted with religion.

But those early songs have never lost the magic.

1958 – SEX EDUCATION – PART 3

The thing about breasts, especially large ones, is that there is a time in your life when they are everything you could want.

I was fifteen and Jillian was a big girl caressed by puppy fat, with a kind face and lovely eyes and black stockings held up by pennies twisted into the tops and enormous breasts that one dark night I was allowed to feel through a thick coat, a double-knit sweater, a school blouse and a cast-iron bra. As the weather grew warmer, Jillian left her coat at home and the wonderful breasts felt less like a pile of laundry and more like my imagination. One very dark night, dark enough to hide my shyness, as we lay by the river I put my hand inside Jillian's sweater and then inside her blouse and then inside her bra and lay perfectly still, waiting for a slap in the face that never came.

At last I was allowed to do it in daylight and Jillian showed me how to undo her bra, though no matter how much I practised I always needed two hands because her bras were powerfully engineered and had four lots of hooks. I was in paradise, lying in the grass by the river, eyes closed, holding her breasts and stroking the nipples that grew hard between my fingers like nuggets of gold, never daring to try for more. She reached up under her skirt and gave me one of the pennies that held her stockings up.

'Tomorrow,' she whispered, 'you can have the other three.'

Wow, tomorrow I will have four-pence, the price of admission to paradise.

And then I went away for the summer to stay with my cousins in Cornwall and found another pair of breasts to adore, older breasts that were smaller, but much more used to being handled and eager to see the light of day, but I was still too scared to go any further. And when I got home Jillian had got fed up waiting and given her virginity to someone else.

1958 – HOW TO BECOME JEWISH & FOREIGN IN LESS THAN FIVE MINUTES

My grandfather was a Polish Jew, or, rather, once upon a time my grandfather had been a Polish Jew. A long time before I was born, he had converted himself into a standard model middle-class Englishman of no specified religion, a conversion so complete that he was left with no hint of an accent and I was too unworldly to see beyond his disguise. He became British to the core, often complaining about all those bloody foreigners that kept coming to live in his adopted land.

His blood is in my blood, only a quarter and most of the time unnoticed, but sometimes I hear certain music and a strange shiver runs up my spine, a sweet comforting sadness that makes you think you're going to cry. There's food too. My mother, who never told me about the Polish secret, took me into a Polish shop once and the air was filled with the fragrance of hundreds of sausages hanging from the ceiling. The smell seemed to have no effect on her, but it made my heart jump with a secret surprise I was too young to understand.

And I didn't know why, apart from the fact that they are delicious.

I think to be Jewish is to embrace misery, to identify with it is something that ties you to all other Jews and sets you apart from the world in a resigned weary place, a place that weighs heavy on your shoulders but a place that you would never choose to leave.

I was seventeen when I saw the red leather boots and they hypnotised me. There were four pairs of them walking ahead of me, three women and a man and I fell in love with their boots. I wanted to rush up and touch them. They were made of soft bright red leather that gathered in gentle folds around the ankles, comfortable boots that had moulded themselves to their owners' feet and become part of them. The four pairs were identical so they were more than a fashion statement. Two more pairs joined them, another man and another woman, and I followed them like a child after the pied piper.

They left the main street and the shops and walked through the back streets of Victorian houses. It was quieter there and I could hear them talking. It wasn't English, very animated with waving hands and laughter.

It was a bit like German or how I imagined Polish or Hungarian might sound, but why the red boots? I wanted to ask them but I was too shy and then they went into a house and it was too late. There was music coming from inside and on the gate a brass plate told me it was 'The Polish Association'.

They were dancing boots and the music drifted over me and I got the shiver feeling and I couldn't move. More people came and one of them spoke to me in Polish.

'I'm sorry, I don't understand,' I said.

'But you are Polish,' he said.

'No, I'm English.'

'No, no you are Polish,' he insisted and spoke to his friends who all nodded in agreement. 'I can see it in your face.'

'Come,' he said and I followed them inside.

There were smells there that embraced me and for reasons I couldn't explain or understand, I felt tears coming up inside me. The man put his arms around me and said again, 'You are Polish.'

I tried to tell him I wasn't, that it was impossible. My whole family was so British, no, not even British. We were English, every single one of us.

'Your grandparent's name, what is that?' he asked.

'Muntz.'

'That is a Polish name.'

'But they're English,' I insisted.

'My boy, Muntz is a Polish name. Smith or Thompson, they are English names, but not Muntz,' he said. 'Go ask them.'

'I...' I started to say. 'It was the boots.'

He took me into a large room, two rooms made into one, where the music was playing and the people in their red boots were dancing, and I was unable to move. The music, the faces, the women's eyes, it all came up inside like a long buried dream. The tears, not sad tears, but something else, raced ahead of the feeling and I could feel them run down my face.

I was so confused. It was all so different from every other part of my life. I didn't even have a half-glimpsed memory to fit to it. If it was a forgotten

dream, it was from before I was born, a dream inherited from ancestors I never knew I had.*

I was embarrassed to be crying but they all seem to think it was wonderful. They said I had discovered my roots but my roots were suburban Ealing, where the shoes were black, not even brown, where the tears were secret, where the ghosts and feelings were locked away in the cupboard under the stairs with the decaying gas-masks and the stirrup pump and the buckets of preserved eggs. My roots were clipped and pruned into tidy shapes, not laughing in red leather boots and swirling embroidered skirts.

'I didn't know you were Polish.'

It was Mary Simon. We sat together at art school. In class, we smiled shyly at each other, not quite sure if we fancied each other or not, so far undecided, but Mary was wearing the red boots and was irresistible.

'Neither did I,' I said.

'Ask them,' she said when I explained about my grandparents, but I was scared to, scared to break their secret, and ashamed of them that they needed to keep it a secret, and frightened that there might have been some important reason for them to do so, and that if I asked them and the secret got broken something terrible might happen.

When I told her about the boots, she laughed and put her legs across mine. There they were, the red leather boots lying in my lap. When I touched them I could feel the warmth of her skin and she looked deep into my eyes and I knew part of me was the same as her and I wanted to throw off her clothes and make love to her right there on the sofa wearing nothing but her boots while the music played and the dancers danced, but of course I didn't. I just blushed and she stroked my cheek and laughed.

'It was a very long time ago,' said my grandmother when I did finally ask her. 'Papa is British now.'

'But...'

'Leave it alone,' she said, angry that I had discovered the lie. 'Papa was a child when he came here, younger than you. He is British. This may not be his homeland but it is his home.'

I wanted to ask her why he was so ashamed of his ancestry that they all had to pretend it didn't exist. That was all I could think of. I didn't know that when his family arrived here as immigrants, to be a Polish Jew was a disadvantage. They were untouchables, confined to the mean streets and a life

---

* *I do hope it was, because I am fascinated by epigenetics.*

of poverty. Nana didn't tell me this, she didn't say that to get on, his family threw away their ancestors and became British, learnt to speak like the British and blend into the background.

When I looked at Papa and thought of the Polish dancers it became obvious, the faces were so alike – dark intense eyes with a shadow of sadness. And when I knew, I didn't know why I'd never seen it before except you don't look. You don't wake up one day and look at your grandfather and say, 'Excuse me Papa, are you a foreigner? Are you Jewish?'

And especially when all his family talked like the BBC and prayed to baby Jesus, you don't. They were as British as our next door neighbours, Mr and Mrs Twistleford-Jones and Mr and Mrs Aranopolis.

Mary sat next to me in drawing class after that. We had something that united us. We were the Poles.

I am only one-quarter Polish, but that didn't matter, Mary and I were related, we were in the same tribe. And because it was only my grandfather I am not Jewish. It has to come from your mother. Unlike her parents, Mary had no accent. She was all Polish and all Jewish, but she was born in England and sounded the same as me. We had become brother and sister so sex was out of the question, but I liked this new thing, being able to confide and talk with no ulterior motives.

Like me, Mary was seventeen and an only child. She lived by herself in a tiny house at the end of a terrace of ten cottages in Haven Lane, at the end of our road, which her father had bought during the war when everyone thought London was going to be bombed out of existence and property was cheap. One by one, he sold the other nine houses until Mary's was the only one left in the family. He gave that to her and moved to the country.

Mary's house was a sanctuary, a safe house in a suburban sea of genteel respectability. Ealing Broadway, London, W5. There were no drunken orgies, no drugs, not even loud music, and no one ever shouted (except the terrifying spastic girl who walked down the road with her thumb in her mouth shouting at everyone and was so scary that I had to cross the road when I saw her coming in case she wanted to talk to me).

Mary and her little house were a sea of calm. Mary floated through the world exuding peace and happiness. She seemed to have no skeletons in cupboards, no broken bits, no lost loves and over the next five or six years whenever I visited her house in Haven Lane to pour out my heart she made me feel peaceful again.

And Haven Lane really was the name of her street, and it's only now that I see it written down I realise how perfect it was.

The haven in Haven Lane.

When things were really bad, she sat me on the floor and sat behind me on the sofa, stroking my hair. Sometimes, she took off my shoes and put her red boots on my feet and talked softly in Polish, words I didn't understand but that sounded so romantic, and bit by bit the world outside went further and further away and I would feel safe again. It made me realise how lonely I had been as a child with no brothers or sisters.

We never talked about becoming lovers but the thought was there, and there were times when we almost reached the point of no return, the greeting kiss lasted just a bit too long or the touch was too smooth, but we knew it would spoil it. We might have had wonderful sex. We have might be more perfectly matched than we ever would with anyone else, but it would have ended and then we'd have both been only children again. What we had then was rare.

We were each other's sanctuary. We could mend each other's broken hearts, except Mary never seemed to have hers broken.

But nothing lasts forever and gradually over the next few years, red boots and stroked hair could no longer keep the devils away. They grew louder and more and more destructive, calmed at first with Librium, calmed at second with extra Librium and so on, but the devils kept getting darker and darker until nothing could send them away.

My grandfather Sydney Muntz – on the right with Nana behind him – and
his brother Samuel Muntz – self-made rich businessmen who made surgical
instruments. If you find yourself getting bits of your body sawn off, my family
may well have made the saw. Their catalogue is amazing, strange and scary.

Hey, I was sixteen already and half the family had changed their name to
Murray. How on earth could I have known they were Polish Jews? I grew
up in my grandparent's house and my grandfather often talked about
Bloody foreigners and called Jaguar cars *A bloody Jewboy's Rolls Royce*.

1958 – SEX EDUCATION – PART 4

Summer ended and so did school uniforms, Brylcreem, short trousers and short-back-and-sides. I went to Ealing Art School and discovered the *Most Wonderful Thing in the Entire History of the World*.

There were actually quite a few *Most Wonderful Things in the Entire History of the World*.

Top of the list were girls – not girls in blue flannel knickers with lace-up shoes and lace-up brains, but Art Student Girls with black stockings and long brown hair and big brown eyes and thick mascara and smiles that could melt your heart from across the room.

Other *Most Wonderful Things* – in no particular order – included:

- The discovery that there were clothes that did not look exactly like the knitted tweed ironed pressed immaculate beige bland stuff every single one of our parents wore. There were these new trousers from America called jeans. We didn't care that they had a girl's name and were stiffer than cardboard until you'd sat in a hot bath in them for a few hours and made them fade a little bit and shrink a lot, and did that quite a few times, we wanted them. At first there was only one shop in London where you could buy them and every time they got some, they sold out in days. On warm summer afternoons there would be a line of us along the river bank at Richmond sitting in the water fading and shrinking our jeans – boys and girls cold, wet and shivering and not being allowed on the bus home because we were dripping water everywhere. The clever ones took other clothes to change into. I went on my motorbike, which meant by the time I got home to Ealing, my jeans were dry, but I had pneumonia.

- Cider and Eel Pie Island.

- Trad jazz and Eel Pie Island.

- Rock and roll, skiffle and The Stones and The Ealing Club.

- Coffee bars – L'Auberge in Richmond, where there was an outside bit you could sit in wet jeans.

- Motorbikes – very cheap and clapped out, but wonderful.

- But of course TOP OF THE LIST was beautiful girls and it is a true fact that almost every Art Student Girl was incredibly beautiful.

College began in September 1958 and in October I was sixteen so, although God said I mustn't, the government said I was allowed to have sex. The lovely Pat with her pear-shaped breasts wasn't going to be sixteen until March 1959 so we agreed to wait until then so we wouldn't go to prison.

This meant we had five months before we could do it. The wait was sort of good because as the weeks went by we grew less shy with each other until we could take quite a lot of our clothes off, not only with the light on, but also with our eyes open.

But when the actual time arrived, I did turn out the light and in the icy darkness with our eyes closed tight, we undressed and slipped beneath the covers to clasp each other like drowning children and discover the shock and excitement of touching someone else's naked body with more than just your hands for the first real time in our lives, an excitement that stays forever, her breasts pressed into my chest, my erection stiff and still in the palm of her stomach. Footsteps and voices passed in the street quite unaware that two lovers were just a few yards away on the verge of one of the greatest moments in history.

'Go on,' Pat said, holding me so tight I could hardly move, but when I finally lay between her rigid thighs and pushed, she stiffened and pulled away.

'Sorry. Do you want me to stop?' I said, half hoping she did. 'We can always do it next weekend. If you want.'

'No, go on,' she whispered.

So I pushed and she backed away and clung tighter and shivered in the darkness and I wanted to see her face, but I was too shy to put the light on or even open my eyes, so I pushed again and she cried out but held me even tighter and I thought I should be kissing her, but I could only concentrate on one thing at a time so I pushed again and then she was crying real tears, but said not to stop so I pushed again, too shy to feel for the right place with my fingers and not sure exactly where the right place was anyway, so I pushed again and she moved a bit and something gave and I almost panicked and stopped but then she pushed back and suddenly it happened and in the next fifteen seconds, which I knew I would remember until the day I died, I opened my eyes and found out why everyone says it's the most wonderful thing in the world and twenty-seven seconds after that I found out that it was

all over and I was worrying about my mother finding blood on the sheets and realised that Pat was crying into the pillow.

'I'm sorry. Did it hurt?'

'No, not really,' she said. 'It's all right, go on.'

'I've done it.'

'Oh.'

'Shall I do it again?'

'No, it's all right. Unless you want to?'

The ritual was over and we were both too shy to speak about it. Still in darkness, we got dressed and only then, when it was safe again and the shivering sweating cold panic had subsided, did I turn the light back on. We hadn't so much made love as floundered together like drowning birds, but even then, because it was our first time, there was something wonderful mixed in with the fear and the tears. And no matter what the women's magazines said about love and being married first, we still respected each other.

When my mother got home we were drinking tea and still shaking and both wondering if we'd really done what we'd really done and I was sure my mother could tell, but of course she couldn't. All that sex stuff was just a rather unpleasant and very distant memory for her, certainly nothing she'd ever done with my stepfather.

'It'll be better next time,' I said, as we stood at the bus stop. 'No one enjoys it the first time.'

Pat didn't say anything but just stood clutching my arm and hiding her face in my coat. Enjoyment had nothing to do with it really, I guessed that would come later. It was the thing itself that mattered then and we'd done that. We were real adults now, true lovers, children no more, mature and wise in the ways of the world and we would probably never be virgins again.

That night I slept with my face pushed into the pillow to catch the fading smell of Pat's hair, her echo, a sweet secret that I wanted to keep forever.

There was, of course, another virginity inside my head that was untouched, but I didn't know that then.

It was better the next time and for a very long time it was always better the next time.

Until Pat got pregnant.

Then I got thrown out of Ealing Art School for refusing to get a haircut*
so I took my portfolio along the road and went to Hammersmith Art School,
where a lot of people had long hair.

The thing was that Ealing wanted to stay in the nineteen-thirties, when
people had known their place in the world.

Pat stayed at Ealing Art School and when I tried to phone her or see
her, she wasn't at home. I wanted to tell her it was all right and we could get
married and I really meant it, and then her best friend Bobbie told me she'd
had a back-street abortion for £10 and it had been twins.

I was devastated and wanted to cry, but I'd forgotten how to.

'If only she'd have let me see her,' I said.

'It wouldn't have made any difference,' Bobbie said.

Pat had moved on. So I moved on and we never saw or even spoke to
each other again.

---

* *Well, it was 1959 – the sixties had yet to be invented.*

GABRIELLE O'REILLY

Gabrielle O'Reilly was half French and half Irish, though you could only tell that from her name. To look at, she was like any other London girl, apart from the glass eye and one breast being quite a bit bigger than the other – though, like her nationality, the eye and the breasts weren't obvious at first glance.

It was Friday night and I was at The Ealing Club, in my usual place with my back to the wall, scanning the room for a familiar face. Like always, there were people I recognised, not friends with names but people who were there every week, people you nodded to. On the little stage at the end of the low tunnel-like room, Manfred Mann was playing rhythm and blues. The drummer's girlfriend was there in her usual place beside the stage, sweetly old-fashioned in this setting with her hair in a tidy plait down below her waist. We'd heard all the songs last week and the week before so we knew the words and could sing along.

'Five – Four – Three – Two – One…' Paul Jones sang and we all joined in.

There were always a few new faces and tonight Gabrielle was one of them. She was standing with her back to the wall too, opposite me on the other side of the narrow room. As the dancing couples between us moved from side to side I caught glimpses of her so small and beautiful, like a tiny white china doll with big green eyes. I'd never seen her there before. She was standing on her own under one of the wall lights, golden in its faint glow. I wanted to go and talk to her, but as always I was nailed to the wall with shyness. She looked at me a couple of times and then when the band stopped playing she walked over.

'I've got a glass eye,' she said before I could even say hello, before she even told me her name or I'd said mine.

I didn't know what to say. I was ready for *Do you have a light?* or *Isn't it loud in here?* But not that.

'I've got a spare one,' she said. 'Look,' and she took a glass ball out of her handbag and polished it on the hem of her sweater. She took my hand in hers and pressed the ball into my palm. With her other hand she folded my fingers over it and smiled, sort of scared. I wanted to look at it but she kept my hand folded closed between hers.

'Now I can see right into your soul,' she said.

I thought that was so beautiful that I wanted to fall in love with her.

The glass eye was as cold as ice but slowly it grew warm in my hand and began to feel heavy. I remember thinking, *If the one she has in is as heavy as that and she tips her head forward, why doesn't it fall out?*

'My name's Gabrielle. You're the only person I've ever told about my eye,' she said. 'But as I think we might be going to spend the rest of our lives together I thought you should know.'

'What?'

'What's your name?'

'Colin.'

'Colin. Colin, do you believe in love at first sight?' she said.

'I suppose.'

'So do I,' she said. 'Even with only one eye. There's something else too.'

'What?'

'My left breast is much bigger than my right one.'

I couldn't see it, but it was enough to make me blush. I could feel the heat of it flushing my face. She was wearing a tight red sweater and her breasts looked beautiful like perfect half globes, big halves of her spare glass eye.

'I've got padding in here,' she said, touching her right breast.

I'd never met anyone so weird and I was glad when the band started playing again so we couldn't hear each other speak.

I gave her the spare eye and she put it back in her bag. I imagined it rolling down to the bottom and getting covered in face cream and fluff. I guessed she'd wash it before she'd use it. And I wondered why would you need a spare? For God's sake, no one's going to steal it, and you wouldn't be likely to forget where you'd put it. Maybe you took it out at night like false teeth. Except a glass eye isn't like teeth, there'd be no risk of swallowing it. I didn't really want to think about it, but it was horribly fascinating. If I'd had a spare eye, I'd have kept it in a black velvet drawstring bag. She nodded towards the door and started to walk off.

Part of me was too scared to move, but she was so pretty and the first girl who had ever chatted me up, so I followed her. Instead of climbing the steps to the street, we turned left and walked along the footpath by the railway lines. It was cold and she took my arm and huddled into me to keep warm. When I looked down at her breasts, I could see her left nipple hard with the cold but where the right one should be, there was nothing, just a smooth curve.

I didn't know what to say and I was too shy to even say that.

Half-back in the real world again, she'd grown quiet too, her bravado gone, her shyness as bad as mine. So we walked in silence, wondering what would happen next. The alley turned away from the railway, working its way between small workshops and at its far end the brightly lit street that was the real world shone bright yellow.

I wanted to stop walking, put my arms round her and kiss her, but I couldn't. I walked as slowly as possible, hoping she'd give me some tiny sign that would help me, but she couldn't.

Then the alley ended and we were back in the real world, in front of the shops and the street lights. Still unable to speak, Gabrielle gripped my arm tighter in a kind of sad desperation. That being her only way of asking me to stay. I wanted to stay and I wanted to say that I was lonely and shy as she was. Her shyness should have given me more confidence, especially after she'd told me all that strange stuff about her eye and her breasts, but it didn't.

We walked past the shops, the street was almost deserted. I could smell her hair and her coat, new smells like a door opening into another life. I wanted so much to put my arms round her and kiss her, but all I had was the familiar feeling of panic.

We passed the coffee bar, the only shop with lit windows. There were a few couples inside and they looked as shy and awkward with each other as we were, frozen like a painting by Edward Hopper. Then the windows were dark again and the shops came to an end. There were a few houses and then we were walking across Ealing Common. It was darker there with just the occasional light half-hidden in the trees. It's easier to hide your shyness when people can't see your face, but the Common wasn't very big and there were more shops and bright lights on the other side. So I had to do something quickly while we were still safe in the shadows.

So I stopped and turned to face her and, *Oh God I'm so scared*.

But she turned to face me and we both shut our eyes and kissed.

It was all right after that. We stopped and sat on a park bench and kissed and cuddled and talked. We'd crossed the dangerous line and were safe and accepted.

She leant in close to me with her face turned down into our laps.

'You must've thought I was some kind of crazy person,' she said.

I shook my head. I did, but she seemed so fragile then that what I felt were waves of tenderness and an all-embracing closeness. It was the same warm feeling of closeness that I used to feel for my cat Tigger when we curled

up in bed together. I'd never felt it for a human before and it was wonderful. Stroking Gabrielle's hair was so much better than stroking Tigger. She smelled better too. This beautiful girl, all wrapped up in my arms, felt like all I could ever want and I just wanted it to stay exactly like that forever.

'I saw you and I wanted to talk to you so much,' she said. 'You've no idea how awful it is to be so shy that it hurts like a big lump of panic inside you.'

'I do. It's like something strangling you so you can't breathe.'

I'd never spoken to anyone about being shy and I had never imagined anyone could have it as badly as I did, especially someone beautiful. And there was this funny little girl, with the glass eye and wonky breasts, as terrified as me. I wanted to hold her and just stay there with her forever in our little circle of safety where we wouldn't ever have to be shy again, but it was getting colder, passing the point where cuddling could keep us warm. It was getting later too and Gabrielle had to catch the bus home. Hand in hand we walked back into the bright streets, linked together until the day we would die.

At home in bed I couldn't sleep. My parents' flat, like always, was as silent as the grave, but less exciting. Across the wide hall my mother and stepfather were lying in their single beds wondering, I hoped, where their lives had gone so wrong. I imagined them both on their backs staring up into the darkness asking themselves if this was all there was. I wanted them to be doing that because it would mean there was hope, but I knew they were probably both fast asleep, backs to each other, the gap between their beds and brains as wide as the ocean, their dreams as bland as their lives.

Now Gabrielle and I were apart, I started panicking. All the fears and insecurities swept back over me. She didn't really fancy me and now we were apart she'd change her mind. I knew she would. A few miles away she couldn't sleep for all the fears and insecurities sweeping back over her, but I didn't know that and if I had, I'd have still been as afraid.

But she hadn't changed her mind and the next day there she was outside the station and we smiled at each other as if we couldn't believe we'd both turned up. We went and sat on the Common and kissed until the cold drove us to the coffee bar. We talked and talked and said nothing. After four days we knew almost as little about each other as we did when we met.

Gabrielle was eighteen. She had a glass eye. Her left breast was bigger than her right – not from anything dangerous, just born that way. Her mother was Irish. Her father was French and she worked at Kodak, processing films.

That was it.

Except that she was slowly going blind in her real eye but was too scared to do anything about it.

I was eighteen. Both my eyes and breasts were real and the same size. My mother was half Polish. My father was absent and I was working in the holidays as a silk-screen printer.

We both lived at home, but soon we would live together.

That was Gabrielle's idea. I didn't like to admit it, but she seemed so grown up and I felt like a child. I lived at home because I was only eighteen and it hadn't occurred to me to do otherwise. She lived at home because until she had met me she had no reason to leave. Neither of us had ever lived anywhere else. I was sure no one would rent us a room because we were so young and we weren't married. It was 1962, but 1962 in Ealing was like 1948 had been in the rest of the world. This bit of London was not swinging, it just hung there limp and musty and refused to look at you.

Gabrielle sorted it out, an upstairs room in a house in the same street as my parents' flat. Our room smelt of mothballs, yet everything in it was moth-eaten. I'd never seen a threadbare carpet before, not in real life and in colour. I'd seen them in those movies where angry young men lived in black and white in another country called Up North, where life was a constant struggle against people like my family. It was dead romantic, like Gabrielle and I were now in a movie too. We had a gas ring, a wardrobe, a sofa, a table with three chairs and a double bed.

And suddenly we'd thrown away the safety barriers that were between us and were face to face in our own movie and I'd never even touched her breasts, the big one or the small one, except through her clothes. We'd only kissed, and now there we were right back at square one with our shyness almost intact.

We closed the curtains and in the half-light we lay on the bed and kissed, completely naked apart from all our clothes, though, of course, we had taken our shoes off. Kissing when you are lying down is so much more erotic than doing it standing up or on a park bench. I suppose it's the thought that you're one step nearer to making love.

'Come on,' she said.

'What?'

She got off the bed, walked across to the door and turned on the light.

'We can't be shy any more,' she said and took off all her clothes in the middle of the room.

I was scared. I could hear my heart beating and feel myself blushing but I took off mine and sat on the edge of the bed.

'Feel,' she said and put my hands on her breasts.

Her left breast was big, more than would fit into my hand. Her right breast was smaller, but not as much as I'd thought it would be. She pulled my face into them. Behind me, there was a gap in the curtains and I imagined my mother standing at her front gate, my old front gate, looking across at us. I hadn't told her I'd left home. I just took a few clothes in a carrier bag while she was in the kitchen. I'd stayed out before. She'd just think I'd hitchhiked down to Brighton again.

I could even take my laundry over and I supposed she'd never know. I thought of her finding a pair of Gabrielle's panties among my clothes. I would have loved to have seen her face, first disbelief, then despair with a prayer and probably ending up with anger. Her anger was always so feeble, it would have been worth it.

Then we were lying down and I couldn't concentrate. I wanted to focus on her body, but hundreds of outside thoughts kept getting in the way. The leak in the fuel line on my motorbike. Every time I replaced it, it seemed to split again. I saw myself in the shop, buying the red rubber tubing. I knew the man behind the counter and he knew me. I think he was called Bill like my aunt. I bought brake levers with knobbly bits on the end last week, like they have on the scrambles bikes. I wanted to get aluminium mudguards next week so everyone won't look at my bike and not know it's one of the old machines they use for telegrams, but now I was going to be paying rent and all that stuff, I probably wouldn't be able to afford them. The sun was shining in through the tree outside and bouncing off the kettle like a little spotlight on the ceiling. I wanted to pull the curtains together.

'I want to close the curtains,' I said.

Gabrielle was lying on top of me and I couldn't reach them.

'I'll do it,' she said, but she didn't.

She opened them wide and before I could do anything she grabbed me and pulled me inside her.

'I want everyone to see us doing it,' she said.

I was out of my depth. My experience had only reached as far as sex in the dark, hiding under the covers for double insulation, the pictures in my head were all fantasies, photographs and memories of half-glimpsed flashes. With the lights on, it had been no more than kisses, and the excitement of stocking tops. So I held on and shut my eyes.

'Open your eyes,' she said. 'Look at me.'

I didn't know where to look, which was ridiculous because my wildest dreams were all coming true right there in front of me. She rolled me onto my side and then my back and all the time I was inside her.

'When you come,' she said, moving up and down and pressing her hands down on my chest, 'I want you to have your eyes wide open.'

It was so scary because she was sort of being like the man, taking charge. And like a man, she came fast and first. She was the first girl I'd ever had sex with who'd had an orgasm. It was so exciting and strange too because all the teenage talk, the teenage imaginings, the hoping and groping, none of it ever mentioned women coming. I suppose somewhere I thought they might but I'd never translated it into reality.

Now this person was screwing her face up and making whimpering noises into my chest and when she lifted her head there were tears running down one side of her face from her single seeing eye.

'I will love you forever,' she said and I knew I'd made a terrible mistake.

I didn't know what the mistake was. It wasn't what she'd said. I wanted to be loved forever more than anything. But then she was moving again and I could feel myself starting to come and mistake was the last word in my mind.

But when I woke up at 3 a.m. I could feel my heart beating in panic. Gabrielle was lying beside me breathing softly, her mouth slightly open, far away in a dreamless sleep.

And her glass eye was wide open.

Her eyelid didn't seem to close when she slept, though it did blink and the faint light caught the glass as she stared sightless at the ceiling.

I lay on my back and stared into the darkness too and there was nothing there. I knew I was broken and that I had to leave before she found out and left me.

A week later I ran away, home to the bland undemanding security and I didn't really know why. Gabrielle was so lovely and so loving, but maybe that was the problem. Maybe I was too unprepared for all this love and closeness, because even though we were in our movie, together in our moth-eaten room, I had this unreasonable fear that it was all going to be taken away from me as punishment for driving my father away. I didn't deserve a happy ending.

Later back home the phone rang. It was Gabrielle and she was drunk.

'You're a fucking bastard,' she said and I couldn't argue.

'I'm going to kill meself,' she said, her accent becoming Irish with the drink. 'I've drunk half a bottle of gin and I'm going back to the fucking room and I'm going to drink the rest and turn on the fucking gas.'

She must have been in the phone box outside Ealing Broadway Station because I could hear a violin playing in the street outside. It was the old man who lost his leg in the war. He put his crutch under his arm and jammed himself against the lamp post while he played the most miserable music you'd ever heard. People threw pennies and sixpences into his hat and I used to wonder how he managed to bend down and pick them up, until one day after the rush of people coming home from work had subsided I saw a Rolls Royce draw up beside him and a smart woman got out, picked up his things and took him away.

Now he was playing for Gabrielle while she cried down the phone and I felt so guilty for not feeling guilty. I should have. She was sweet and kind and I had deserted her, but it all seemed unreal. We were only together a week and I told myself that no one could fall in love so much in a week that they would kill themselves.

I told myself that, but I didn't believe it.

I tried to talk her out of it, tell her to be calm, tell her to stay put and I'd be there in five minutes, but she screamed and said if I ever went near her again she'd say I raped her and smash the gin bottle in my face.

I sat outside my house and waited for her to come up the road, but she didn't, so I told myself she was only bluffing and she'd probably gone home to her parents.

Three months later I found out what had happened. I met her one night in The Ealing Club and she told me, enough time having passed for us to be kind of friends once more and even become lovers again for a little while, until her sight became so weak that she fled to the security of her family's village in Ireland and the protection they offered.

She had gone back to the room, but she was so drunk that when she turned on the gas, she forgot to close the windows or put money in the gas meter. She drank the rest of the gin took all her clothes off and then passed out. Later in the afternoon, her cousin came round, sent by her mother to persuade her to stop living in sin and go back home. The cousin in his white Aran sweater, a good boy who was training for the priesthood, found Gabrielle naked on the floor and in carrying her to the bed, found himself strangely aroused in an area he had previously given little thought to, and so took advantage of the situation to lose his virginity and vocation. When Gabrielle came to, she came too, and then gave him a black eye.

That Christmas a card arrived from Ireland saying she had married her cousin and they were expecting 'a happy event'.

SHOCK TREATMENT

When I was a little boy, as well as the ones on the wall, there were some light switches that hung down from the ceiling at the end of a cloth-covered flex with a button at the bottom. There was one above my bed so you didn't have to get out of bed to turn the light out.

I'm not sure why, but I liked to stand at the head of my bed on the pillow and press the button to make the light go on and off over and over again. It drove my mother crazy, which is probably why I did it.

'If you keep doing that,' she said, 'you'll get an electric shock.'

'No I won't,' I insisted.

Then I got an electric shock and it threw me against the end of the bed and my grandfather had to go and mend the fuse.

****

Many years later up in Cumbria my accountant had bought some of my decorated tiles and I was sticking them up in his laundry. This meant moving a power point so I told him to turn off the electricity, which he did except for the solitary switch hidden next to the fuse box. I sliced through a thick cable with my Stanley knife and sat down with a bang hard enough to get a bruise. My accountant, white with the thought of legal proceedings, went to make me a strong cup of tea, but some idiot had turned the electricity off. It was about ten minutes before we noticed the kettle wasn't boiling.

1960 – WIVES – PART 1

Susan was the most beautiful girl I had ever seen up close.
She was actually beautiful from any distance, even when she was out of sight because I could still see her face when I shut my eyes.

We were eighteen and pregnant when we got married. We knew it was going to happen. The rhythm method works, but it relies on self-control and mathematics and we weren't much good at either of them.

I'm still not.

So on that day when we were alone in her parent's house with their big double bed, on one of the dangerous days when it was too hot to keep all our clothes on and oh what the hell, life's too short, and it had never felt as great as it did that day – far too good to come out in time. So we knew what could happen.

And it did.

We learned that two wrongs don't so much make a right as make a baby.

We learned a lot later on, after the parental fury had calmed down and we were married and happy living in our own world, that Susan's parents had also made the same discovery and produced her. And although no one would ever admit it or even talk about it, I still think Susan's father, who looked and thought like a goldfish and had two more daughters who looked and thought like goldfish, could never have fathered someone as beautiful and different as my wife. No one will ever know, which means we can believe whatever truth we want.

Our own world was wonderful in a romantic two-roomed attic at the top of a Victorian house in Ealing, three miles from where I was born, and where our cat tried to drag a complaining pigeon up the two flights of stairs but never got more than three steps before the pigeon flapped its wings and they fell down two steps. Much to the cat's complaining, I took the pigeon up onto the roof and it flew away tired, but surviving.

To show his disapproval, my stepfather, Claude Baines Thompson, wore his Harris Tweed gardening jacket with the leather elbow patches and sandals to our wedding. I should have admired that because it was probably the only moment of rebellion in his entire life.

I went off to work silk-screen printing each day on my twelve quid Lambretta scooter while my wife looked after our daughter, Charlotte. I worked all day at my bench next to Adam Faith at his bench, who was Terry in those days and who left a few weeks later and then came back in a red sports car with a beautiful starlet and told us he was going to be on Sunday Night at the London Palladium, which was like the Nobel Prize. I printed the same thing all day and every day for three months – fluorescent red and blue approved by the Gas Council stickers – twenty-four to a sheet until I had fluorescent red and blue dots dancing in my eyes. But in those days there was lots of work so I went to another screen-printing shop where we printed posh stuff on posh paper for posh art magazines. And one by one the five other printers who were my age went away to get regimented, shaved, shorn and adjusted for an unquestioning life of straight lines in the army and then back to work printing two years later with the sparkle gone from their eyes and all ready for World War Three.

I was terrified as the weeks went by because I knew I would spend two years locked up for refusing to follow the rules. But then a miracle happened and National Service ended and I was born just late enough to miss it.

Under the attic roof the winter passed with warm nights under musty eiderdowns until the baby grew too large for us to make love. Snow fell and covered the peeling paint. Frost decorated the window panes with ferns of ice, but the sun was still shining.

March came and the baby was supposed to arrive but it didn't. Susan had grown larger and larger, puffing and panting slower and slower up the narrow stairs to the flat.

A week passed and still nothing happened until one day I came home from work with half a bottle of gin in my pocket.

'You look tired,' I said. 'Have some gin.'

'Gosh, it's ages since I had a drink.'

Susan sat by the tiny gas fire, large and warm. Her face had grown round in the last few weeks of her pregnancy but she had lost none of her beauty.

'Where did you get it?' she said, knowing we didn't have the money to buy gin.

I'd stolen it from the back of a filing cabinet at work but I told Susan I'd won it off my workmates at cards.

'My feet are killing me,' she said. 'They said at the clinic that it's like walking round with fifteen bags of sugar tied round your middle.'

'Why don't you have a nice hot bath?' I suggested.

'Do you think it's a good idea?'

The bathroom was downstairs on the floor below and we shared it with three other lots of tenants. I ran the water until the room was full of steam and so warm that I suddenly wanted to make love to Susan but we hadn't dared to for the past three weeks, so I sat with my back to the taps clutching my knees while Susan lay vastly pregnant in front of me, finishing the gin.

Four hours later she cried out in her sleep and I stumbled downstairs to the pay-phone to get the ambulance that carried us through the March fog to the hospital.

Two hours later I was turned out into the cold and five hours later when I was at work, Susan gave birth to Charlotte.

Everything was perfect. Susan and I spent a happy fifteen months on the edge of a career and mortgage, but then something broke inside my head.

In those days no one said *It doesn't get any better than this* – and it didn't. And, of course, that meant it was too good to last.

And it didn't.

It all fell to bits in a terrible, painful, terrifyingly confusing way, made a thousand times worse by having no sense or explanation or reason or visible end or solution or help. No one had done anything to make it broken and no one could say why or how it had.

I fell slowly and relentlessly into a deep dark hole of unrelieved depression. And then I spent three years sitting in the hole looking up at the sky until I had a crick in my neck and not once did the blue bird fly over, though a bit of me never stopped believing it would.

In those days which were 1962 the only known cure for depression was *Snap Out of It*. It still is, though slightly less, a popular treatment.

Which is amazing, considering the millions of people who have discovered it doesn't work.

But I was lucky. I had a doctor who didn't say that. She gave me pills – Librium three a day which became six a day and then nine and more, until they didn't work any more.

RUNNING AWAY – PART 1

Sue and Charlotte went back to her mother's.
The sun went out with a bang a week ago, leaving a total eclipse in my head. I had Librium for breakfast, Librium for lunch and Librium for dinner. In the gloom of our sad flat nothing moved any more. The cat fell off the roof and crawled away to die. All the promise that was going to fill our entire future had gone and I couldn't see any hope for more.

So I decided to go to 'Abroad'. I put two pairs of jeans and a few other clothes in a small holdall with the Penguin book of Chinese verse and Joyce Cary's *The Horse's Mouth* and walked away.

I took the train to the far side of London and then hitchhiked down to Dover. It was easy getting lifts in those days. Hitchhikers were a bit of a novelty and I reached Dover in less than three hours, the last twenty miles hanging on for dear life on the back of a Triumph Bonneville.

There were no ferries from Dover that day so the motorbike took me to Folkestone. It was the first time I'd ever visited 'Abroad'. It was so exciting that I nearly threw my Librium into the English Channel.

In Boulogne I got a lift from a real Frenchman in a real French car on the way to the real French Paris. I couldn't understand a word he said except 'bye bye' when he dropped me in the middle of nowhere at ten o'clock at night.

Things were a bit less great then. It really was nowhere, no houses, no lights, just a long dark road with fields and trees, no traffic at all and a thick mist crawling over everything.

I had no map, and no torch to read it by if I'd had one and I was cold, but it was still exciting. I tried to sleep in a graveyard but the cold kept me awake so I kept on walking and after ten minutes a car came along and stopped.

Three crazy, drunk Italians on holiday took me to a nightclub in Amiens. I didn't want to go in because I only had twelve pounds to live on forever and they could've drunk that in five minutes. So I started walking again and at one in the morning a man stopped and took me into Paris.

Wow, I was in Paris. I couldn't believe it. I felt great. I drank some coffee and bought some bread and discovered the French I had been learning at school for over ten years had absolutely nothing to do with whatever it was they spoke in France and no one had the slightest interest in 'the fountain pen of my aunt'.

But I'd already decided I wasn't going to stay in France. I'd got to Paris so easily, I decided I'd go on to Spain. I knew someone who'd been there and he'd said it was great.

So I started hitchhiking again but this time the cars were going so fast no one would stop. But at last someone did.

Oh shit, it's a police car and two French policemen are coming towards me pointing revolvers at my head.

Oh shit.

I dropped my bag and put my hands up. They were both shouting at me, a hundred words a minute. They grabbed my bag and pushed me against the car. They frisked me like in the movies and in all their shouting I understood two words.

I was an Algerian bastard – well, I did have a leather jacket and a suntan.

The cops who had been frisking me pulled out my passport and instantly they were smiling and laughing and slapping me on the back. I wasn't an Algerian bastard after all.

I was a dumb English kid. How was I to know it was illegal to hitchhike on the freeway?

And because I was just a dumb English kid they would help me. First we would go to the police station where some of them spoke English and we would have coffee and croissants.

And when we had finished our coffee and croissants we got back in the police car and drove to the end of the freeway, where they made cars pull over until they found one going almost all the way to the Spanish border.

The driver was so relieved the cops weren't booking him for something that he was only too happy to give me a lift. I got a lift the final few kilometres from an Englishman who made me get out and walk the last bit because he didn't want the border police to see him with anyone.

He left his car in some trees and told me to walk on ahead. And there I was in Spain – London to the Spanish border in twenty-four hours.

I fell asleep on a bench in the station and waited for the train to Barcelona. I went on the boat to Ibiza in steerage, which was incredibly cheap, but meant you were locked in a windowless hold and couldn't go up on deck. It was so cheap, I didn't care and I slept most of the journey on some bales of canvas.

As the boat coasted into port someone unlocked the door and pointed up the stairs. It was night-time. The sky was full of stars. There were at least twice as many as we had in England and the air was hotter

than I'd ever felt air before. I had arrived in paradise and I walked up the gang-plank with a stupid big grin all over my face. It was all just so amazing – little streets with white-washed houses, beautiful sun-tanned people in bright cafés and the exotic smells of food and warm bodies. It was so romantic and so different from the dull grey world I'd come from. Why had I never gone to 'Abroad' before?

I felt as if I'd come home, that this was where I was supposed to have been all my life. I walked to the edge of the town and lay on the grass above the sea, staring at the moon. It all felt so simple and easy I wanted to cry. I fell asleep inside a dream and woke up six hours later as a group of men were shitting among the rocks.

So much for beauty, and this was when Ibiza *was* beautiful and the only foreigners were a few rich American kids and the odd temporary passer-through like me.

I took the small open boat across to the little island of Formentera. It was perfect. There was almost nothing here, a few houses, some salt pans and a shop that rented me a room for two shillings a day. Another two shillings for food and my ten pounds would last for ages. The fare home was something I would worry about later.

I washed my clothes under a tap, sat in the sea, ate bread, tomatoes and sardines and lay in the sun and planned the rest of my life.

Leaving people aside, there had only been one future in my mind for as long as I could remember. I was going to spend my life painting. It would be difficult. It would be a struggle, but I was still young enough to think it was all romantic. I thought I should probably try to live in Paris, but England would do as long as I could live in a garret with a sloping roof and good north light and an endless stream of olive-skinned models with long brown hair who would adore me for my genius.

Oh shit. I had all that in Ealing with Sue and I fucked it up.

Susan came back into my head and I was overwhelmed with home-sickness and missing her. I'd been on Formentera for two weeks. I'd re-read *The Horse's Mouth* again and I still had six pounds left.

Now Susan was calling to me, but so was the golden sand and the endless sunshine and the peace and quiet. I could stay at least another week and still have enough to get me back home. So I wrote to Sue and lay back in the sunshine. Except the one week became two and a bit and by then I only had enough money to get back to Barcelona, but no further.

So I went back into the windowless hold and arrived on the mainland on an early Monday morning with the first hint of autumn in the air. I went to the British Embassy and started to explain why I had to get home to my wife and daughter.

They didn't want explanations. They'd heard all of them before. All they wanted was my passport, which they filled with big red stamps so it would be confiscated the minute I reached Dover. They gave me some money for food and a third-class train ticket from Barcelona to Dover and said that when I paid them back, they'd return my passport. Fair enough.

It was nice sitting by the train window watching France fly by. I always feel comfortable in trains. There's the promise of adventure, and a warm feeling of sad solitude. I ate my bread and cheese, drank my water and stared out of the window. Nobody spoke to me for the whole journey, not even the sullen ticket inspector, who just held out his clippers and grunted. I hitched back to London, to Sue and Charlotte, who were waiting for me in the ground-floor flat of the house where we'd first lived in the attic.

We slept wrapped in each other's arms, but we both knew it was over. There was no reason for it to be. I think we still loved each other, but something was broken and we were too young to know how to mend it. We tried so hard. Maybe we tried too hard. I got shingles around my waist and helpful friends told me if they joined up I would die. The itching drove me crazy and every day we drifted helplessly further and further apart.

I was now taking fifteen Librium a day. The broken thing was in my head.

The sun had stayed behind in Formentera.

One evening my doctor came and drove me across London in her own car past all the people hurrying home from work like I'd been doing until a few months before. The light withered, night time began and we reached the hospital, drove through the open gates past a nodding man and up to a darkened door. The doctor pressed the horn and the door opened, spilling false sunshine onto the gravel. Two men in white coats came out and took me inside. The lovely doctor retouched her make-up in the little mirror behind the sun visor and went back to her cocktail party, though by the time she got there all the canapés had gone.

I climbed into bed and fell asleep without realising exactly where I was.

All I knew was that my beautiful wife and child were somewhere else and I was behind bars. I so wished I could remember how to cry.

THINGS THAT GOT BROKEN

1950 – LUDLOW – my skull. I fell backwards off a tricycle onto the pointed concrete edge of a path. My mother walked me up the road to the hospital with a wet towel on my head. When we got there, the towel was completely red and little rivers of blood were running down my neck. It was very exciting and, as far as I can remember, quite painless.

All the doctors were at the races so I didn't get x-rays or stitches, just three sticking plasters and a bandage right round my head, which I could stick chicken feathers into and be a red-Indian. Then we walked back down the hill and I got ice-cream. From that day on I had a little bald spot hidden under my hair. Now, the little bald spot is hidden under a bigger bald spot.

1950 – EALING – my jaw. I fell onto a brass fender at school. That did hurt a lot, especially when I went to a dentist's appointment that very afternoon and screamed every time he touched my mouth.

'Don't be such a baby,' said my mother.

'I think there might be something wrong,' said the dentist when I told him about the brass fender. This time there were doctors and nurses at the hospital so I got an x-ray. My jaw was broken. Mummy didn't say sorry.

OTHER BROKEN THINGS INCLUDE – promises, hopefully not too many serious ones, though I suppose two lots of 'til-death-do-us-part wedding vows, a terminated pregnancy and fleeing to the other side of the world are pretty big damaging things to do to people. I did my best, but I hadn't had any experience of a father or a mother with real feelings to learn from so I don't think I was a very good at it.

Sorry.

POSTSCRIPT – 1

HOW DO YOU GET DEPRESSION?

I grew up in a very conservative world. There were only two species in my world – us and poor people, and the poor people were basically us with no money and beans on toast instead of roast beef and Yorkshire pudding. So there was really just one species.

Ties – very neat haircuts – shiny shoes – church on Sundays – total obedience to everything – a quick one-way chat with Jesus and his dad before bed and then sleep with your hands above the covers.

Designed so perfectly that you never needed to think about anything. Groundhog Day forever and ever amen.

Lovely.

And comfortable.

And simple.

Except when I was eleven, it all got muddled up.

My mother married a piece of wood and I discovered something under the covers and that if you played with it, it got stiff and exciting and was probably very naughty and, allegedly, could even make you go blind, but it was a risk worth taking.

So when I was eleven, the edges began to fray and they kept fraying until by the time I was sixteen, life had a fringe.

And behind the fringe there was another world full of everything I'd ever wanted. Except that in my cotton wool lined box I had never known it even existed. Until then it had all just been an abstract possibility. At sixteen I discovered that making sex a reality was the most exciting, wonderful, indescribable journey to a paradise that nothing could ever come close to. There was love too. That was like adding marzipan and thick icing and I wanted as much as I could get.

There was freedom too, and cigarettes and chips, which I had never had before because my grannie thought they were common, and drink and in between all of that more sex and the knowledge that finally at long last someone had opened the curtains and the sun was going to shine in forever.

And that is how and why you get depression.

hen I was a child, I fitted in perfectly. Then I got bigger, but the box stayed the same size."

This bit is for me and my grandson because it's about Asperger's, which isn't called Asperger's any more, and we've both got it. Apparently OR NOT

I don't think I had it when I was a little boy because I was really, really good all the time apart from wetting the bed a lot, but I don't think you have to have Asperger's to do that. In fact I don't think I got it until I was quite old, except everyone says you have to be born with it, but that can't be right because it wasn't invented until I was two years old. So I think I probably caught it somewhere like off a lavatory seat or from a meat pie.

People who have Asperger's are often called **ASPIES** and people who don't have Asperger's are called **NEUROTYPICALS**.
I don't like either of those words, so, people with Asperger's will be called **ME** or **US** and people without Asperger's will be called **THEY** or **THEM**.

Wherever you go you will find out there are millions and millions of RULES. Lot of them are stupid. Lots of them are pointless, useless and completely wrong. The thing is that most of the rules were made up by **THEM** and not **US** to make **THEIR** lives easier and the trouble is that a lot of their rules makes **OUR** lives more difficul

WHAT IS ASPERGER'S?

THIS is what the DICTIONARY says -

Asperger's syndrome | ˈaspəːɡəz, ˈaspəːdʒəz | (also **Asperger** syndrome)

noun [mass noun]

developmental disorder related to autism and characterized by awkwardness in social interaction, pedantry in speech, and preoccupation with very narrow interests.

ORIGIN named after Hans Asperger (1906–80), the Austrian psychiatrist who described the condition in 1944.

yeah, yeah, very funny
IT'S NOT THIS

But, of course, the answer is not that simple because at different times it's had different names -

200 YEARS AGO It was called **BEING POSSESSED BY EVIL SPIRITS.**

WHEN I WAS A LITTLE BOY It was called **BEING NAUGHTY.**

THEN it was called **ASPERGER'S SYNDROME.**

AND EVERYONE WAS HAPPY WITH THAT UNTIL SOME VERY IMPORTANT COMMITTEE decided that **THEY** had to change the name because they were **VERY IMPORTANT**. So now we don't have **ASPERGER'S** any more. **NOW WE HAVE ASD** - which stands for **AUTISM SPECTRUM DISORDER** and is much too complicated.

ere's an **INTERESTING NOTE** that not many people know. Dr Asperger had an assistant called Heinrich Bottom. Dr Asperger hadn't been so self-important, he might have named his syndrome after his assistant and now, **WE** ould all be suffering from **BOTTOM'S**, which only goes to show that sometimes it is good to be selfish.

RULE #1

WE ARE

NOT

BROKEN OR BETTER
OR WORSE

Rule One is not actually a rule, but it should be because it is **THE MOST IMPORTANT** thing and it is so **IMPORTANT** that **EVERYONE** SHOULD LEARN IT.

THEY always say 'Everyone is different', which isn't true because most of **THEM** are all the same as each other and the last thing they actually want is to be **DIFFERENT**. They all want to be **EXACTLY** the same as each other, but with a bit more money.

And it's because **WE ArE DIFFEReNT** that **THEY** have a problem with **US**. **THEY** cannot understand **US** and **THEY** cannot control or change **US** even though they keep trying and it drives **THEM** mad, especially as **THEY** think **WE** will be 'better' if **WE** change, which **WE** probably won't.

ANYWaY, as it says on the page before this one **WE** are **NOT BROKEN.** In fact **WE** are

SPECIAL

...ome of **THEM** will say that you are a **SPECIAL NEeDS** person. ...his is what the dictionary says **SPECIAL** means —

See, I told you so.

special
adjective
1 better, greater, or otherwise different from what is usual: *they always made a special effort at Christmas.*
• exceptionally good or pleasant: *he's a very special person.*

We'll come back to **SPECIAL NEEDS** later.

RULE #2

I'M NOT SURE, BUT THIS MIGHT BE THE MOST IMPORTANT RULE

DON'T ASK QUESTIONS

BACON

WHY NOT?? WHY? WHAT? WHY? I MEAN WHY NOT? WHY NOT? WHEN?

THE NEXT PAGE WILL TELL YOU

THIS IS WHY IT'S MUCH EASIER IF WE DON'T

ASK QUESTIONS

THIS IS SORT OF SERIOUS.

Because **OUR BRAINS** work at one million miles an hour, **WE** are usually thinking about a lot of things at the same time. So when **WE** ask a question, quite often **WE** are thinking about something completely different by the time **THEY** answer **THE QUESTION**. This means that, although the answer goes into **OUR HEADS**, it gets put in a box with thousands of other things that have nothing to do with it. So quite often **WE** will have to ask exactly the same question again – and again – and maybe again. Sometimes it might be one hour later. Sometimes a week. For some reason this **DRIVES THEM MAD** and **THEY** find it **IMPOSSIBLE** to just say the answer again, which would take about two seconds. Instead, **THEY** get **ANGRY** and say, '**I already told you that**,' and a lot of other stuff and so quite often the answer itself is all tangled up in a lot of other words, which means it gets lost again.

Sometimes the answer isn't quite right. The right answer to the question '**When are we going?**' is not, '**tomorrow**.' The right answer is '**ten o'clock tomorrow morning**.' **WE** need to know exactly when to get our brains organised, and not just when to put **OUR** coats on. **AND WE NEED TO KNOW** what is going to happen if **WE** don't go at ten o'clock. That is **REALLY IMPORTANT**.

THERE ARE TWO THINGS WE CAN DO AND THEY ARE BOTH REALLY DIFFICULT

1 Try really, really hard to concentrate and listen to every single world THEY are saying and try and remember them in the same order they said them and put them inside your head where you can find them again and not on that shelf back there with the box of Christmas decorations that we looked everywhere for last year and stop looking at that thing outside the window, which is very interesting, especially the way it, no, no, concentrate, what's that on the back of your finger, is it a cut or is it just an ink mark no, hang on, no just a minute, yes, what, oh look at that dog out there I wonder what its name, is it time to go home yet?
Oh look, it's raining.
See, it's really hard isn't it?

I wish I had a dog like that

Actually, I have!

2 There isn't a second thing really, except not asking the question in the first place and THAT IS PROBABLY IMPOSSIBLE.

Here is some more QUESTION stuff

MORE QUESTION STUFF

SOMETIMES we ask a question a bit too quickly, which means if we thought about it for a few seconds we would realise that the answer is obvious. **FOR EXAMPLE** - Grass is green so we don't need to ask 'What colour is the grass?'

EXCEPT that if the grass is dead, then it might be yellow or white or brown or some other colour and if someone had dropped some paint on the grass it could be any colour so 'What colour is the grass?' is actually not a very good example.

AND SOMETIMES we ask a question when we already know the answer, but we want someone else to tell us the same answer. This is not because we think we might have got the answer wrong, but just to reassure us.

THE TROUBLE IS THAT THERE ARE ALWAYS MORE QUESTIONS

Some things that **THEY** might find **REALLY EASY** **WE** often find **REALLY DIFFICULT.**

The thing that is the **HARDEST** to do is quite **WEIRD** and **I** don't understand it.
I can't **LOOK YOU IN THE EYE. WHY** on earth is that?
GOOGLE just says that -

IT HURTS.

AND IT DOES - SORT OF INSIDE YOUR HEAD RIGHT BEHIND YOUR EYES, BUT I DON'T KNOW WHY.

The trouble is that **THEY** often think that **WE** are not listening to **THEM** when **WE** are. Unless of course **THEY'RE** being really **BORING**, in which case **NO ONE** would want to listen to **THEM**, but that's different.

SOME OTHER THINGS THAT ARE REALLY DIFFICULT

Some people are sitting around talking and **YOU** want to say something and it's **REALLY IMPORTANT** because it's something that will tell **THEM** all something **REALLY USEFUL** about the thing **THEY** are talking about, **BUT** there aren't any gaps in the talking where **YOU** can add the thing **YOU** want to say.

SO there are **TWO** things **YOU** can do.

1 - **YOU** can **INTERRUPT**, which will probably make **THEM** **CROSS** even though **YOU** have told **THEM** something really good.

2 - **YOU** can just not say anything, which is **VERY STRESSFUL**.

WE are **ALWAYS** told that **WE** must **NEVER** tell **LIES**. So when someone asks us if **THEY** look nice when **THEY** look **AWFUL** why are **WE** supposed **LIE**?

THEY don't seem to mind if things don't work properly or are **REALLY DIFFICULT** to use, but **WE** know that sort of thing is **ReALLY, ReaLLY IMPORTANT.**

Some of these things are not here because they don't work properly, but just because **I HATE THEM** and this is **MY** book so I can put them in.

SO IF I WAS KING OF THE WORLD, THESE THINGS WOULD BE
AGAINST THE LAW.

PARSNIPS - EVIL, REVOLTING AND DISGUSTING, INVENTED BY THE DEVIL IN 1342 - BANNED IN EVERY CIVILISED PLANET THROUGHOUT THE GALAXY EXCEPT EARTH.

Those **HORRIBLE** little plastic things you get on bags of bread and veggies

TURNIPS - JUST AS EVIL AS PARSNIPS. SO WHAT DO WE LEARN FROM THIS? ALL VEGETABLES THAT END WITH 'NIPS' ARE VERY, VERY, BAD.

Cardigans are jolly comfortable

'NIPS' IS NOT THE ONLY BAD ENDING. YOU SHOULD ALSO KEEP AWAY FROM ANY FOOD ENDING WITH 'MITE'.

EARS WITH HAIR GROWING OUT OF THEM :
MOUSTACHES :
TROUSERS THAT REACH YOUR ARMPITS :
CARDIGANS :
BEIGE :

AND whoever designed or even uses this typeface should go to jail FOREVER or EVEN LONGER.

I bet **YOU** can think of a lot more things that should be **BANNED.**

ARE WE THERE YET?

WHAT **THEY** SAY

'Are we there yet?'

'Are we ther

'Are we ther

'Are we there yet?'

'Are we

'Are we

'Are we there yet?'

'Are w

'Are w

'Are we there yet?'

WHAT **WE** SAY

'ARE WE THERE YET?'

'MUM, HE'S PLAYING WITH IT AGAIN.'

'WILL they STILL BE open when we get there?'

'ARE YOU SURE?'

'will there be any bacon left?'

'MUM, she keeps pointing at me.'

'I NEED TO PEE.'

'Dad, what are those horses doing?'

'MUM, HE'S JUST BEEN SICK.'

AGAIN. .

Of course everyone will say 'But ALL children do that, not just Asperger's.' And this is true.
So what do we learn from that? **ALL CHILDREN** are a bit **ASPERGERY.**

1963 – LOONY BIN No. 1

At first I noticed nothing beyond the weak blue light on the ceiling. No fear, no joy, no self-pity nor anger, no reaction to the cries and screams that rang out near and far through the night.

All aches, all pains, all feelings had gone and in their place an empty distance and a sedated numbness so heavy that my brain hung inside my head in suspended animation.

My body moved where it was told to go, ate, washed, shaved with a very safe safety razor that a nurse locked with a key, moved some more, and then went to bed in a room of twenty beds.

That was the day, the next day and the day after too. The air smelt stale as if it had been trapped inside the grey corridors forever. It tasted as if it had been breathed in and out a thousand times by long-dead lungs, like a bouquet of rotten flowers, a smell of life worse than death.

Horrible faces pulled apart by real madness seemed to jump out from every doorway. Some wore smiles more terrifying than hatred, but most were flat and empty like my own, held down with drugs.

As the other patients looked through me, I looked through them with a blank fog that covered my eyes. It was like looking into a mirror and finding you'd been given a new face.

A week passed before I realised that I was in a lunatic asylum. No one came to see me or wrote or telephoned. Although it was surrounded by the South London suburban streets of Tooting, Springfield Hospital felt like it was in another world. On that first day, in dead men's pyjamas, I curled up into a small ball under the blankets and vanished. Although it was just over the fence, the real world was miles away and parts of me were still out there, scattered across the city in the memories of others, lost to me forever.

Distant conversations and even laughter slipped through my head unrecorded. It grew dark and through little dusty panes of smash-proof glass the dirty sun fell wearily down a hundred yards away over the tall fence, across suburban gardens that might as well have been on the other side of the universe. Beyond the gardens, people returned from work to little rows of tidy houses.

It seemed like the whole world was living lives of quiet desperation.

The difference being, some of us coped better than others. Some roared against the machine while most lay down and let it roll over them.

Out there, they sat down to their suppers and evenings by the fire. Televisions flashed and flickered their grey lights through French windows onto neat green lawns.

Why couldn't I have been neat and green?

Tired children refused to sleep while their tired mothers stood wearily at kitchen sinks, wishing they could. Dogs curled up at their masters' feet and dreamt their dreams with twitching feet and eyes that flickered behind closed lids.

The glass, some cold evening air and the high wire fence were all that lay between madness and the outside world. Out there, what the dogs did at their masters' feet, some humans did in Springfield. In padlocked rooms incurable minds were transformed into vegetables and Gods lay transfixed in time, barely more than an arm's length from sanity or existence. Curled up on iron beds, they slept with eyes wide open, twitching through their dreams like the dogs, but with no happiness when they woke up.

Out there, in the houses, grey hair appeared as people lived and loved and survived. Their children grew up and had children of their own and went to live in houses of their own with maybe one in ten thousand of them ending up in here where everything stood still. People aged like compost, their colours faded, their hopes withered and their worst dreams became cruel reality, but unlike compost they didn't metamorphose into anything useful.

I saw nothing through the glass. My own sun had sunk far below the horizon. Deep down in the back of my head, I knew that it would rise again though when and for how long I couldn't guess. Nor did I know if it would sink again or stay up in the sky. Locked in the ward at night, I lay on my back with my blurred eyes focused on that weak blue light that stayed on twenty-four hours a day. After two weeks a Welsh psychiatrist came and listened to my heart.

'Well, boy, what are you doing here?' he said.

'I don't know.'

'You don't know? You don't know? Well if you don't know, how can you expect me to know?'

'Can I have my clothes back?' I said.

'Of course you can, boy. Don't think we were going to let you lie about in bed all day, do you?' the doctor said, and went off to humiliate someone else.

Then the first emotion came back into my empty head. And it was hatred for the patronising bastard who was supposed to be helping me. Later I wondered if that was part of the treatment, bad cop, bad cop but I don't think it was. I think he really was a patronising bastard.

Later still I learned that this doctor had an arm full of needle holes and a prison record for trying to strangle his wife, and behind triple-locked doors he fucked the triple-drugged lunatics. The blind led the guide dogs.

The sadness of leaving Susan slipped away, leaving guilt at her pain and the old groundless depression that had haunted me now for more than a year. Drugged days blurred together with no cures and no change. Around me people came and went. After little more than a rest, some were sent home. One or two left and threw themselves under buses or trains or handfuls of sleeping pills. A man who had slept in the bed next to mine wished us all a happy goodbye then went home and burnt himself to death with petrol in a last attempt to bring some warmth into his life. And a few were sent in the other direction into the heart of the asylum, behind double sets of double-locked doors, to see out their days in the land of the barely living dead.

Most, like me, were sent into wards where the doors were only locked at night. I fell into the daily routine. Every morning I joined the queue for the suicide-proof razor. Ten people shaved and then a nurse unlocked it and put in a new blade. Three times a day after meals I lined up for drugs. Two nurses wheeled a trolley down the line and handed out numbness apathy in different coloured pills. One nurse with the pills and water and one nurse with her surgical gloved fingers in your mouth to make sure you'd swallowed them. For some patients, it was the highlight of their day, especially the rubber gloves.

No one was exempt.

The days became weeks and, cut off from the demands of the real world, my depression began to lift. From deep inside my heart an anger began to emerge, an unspecified, unreasoned anger. I didn't feel anger at the depression I had been cursed with. That was just how things were.

Even in my days of deepest despair I never thought *Why me?*

Sometimes, when suicide taunted me, I wished I could be normal, but I told myself, as all manic-depressives do, that without the depths I couldn't have the highs and that the highs could be so wonderful they were a rare privilege denied to the common man. Sometimes this was true. Most of the time it was rubbish.

Some people went into Springfield with an apathy that blossomed and grew into complete silence, leaving them prematurely old and as helpless as

babies. Half the inmates were like that, institutionalised and so dead that they had to be led and fed. The oldest, loveless and abandoned, incontinent and unknown, slipped quietly into death, often with a little discreet help.

I used to wonder if, behind some of the silent vacant stares, there were violent torments going on, or they really were just vegetables. No one could ever know for certain what was happening inside their heads.

Maybe they'd simply forgotten how to speak or just used up all their words. Or maybe they just had nothing to say. And why was it mostly the women who seem to be so silent? Others, only part-way there, wandered the grey-tiled corridors in wide-awake dreams and fabulous fantasies.

The anger that grew inside me saved me. It brought with it the shock of realising that I was shut up in a real lunatic asylum.

'What am I doing here?'

'You tell me, boy,' the doctor said at our second meeting.

'Well, I suppose there was nowhere else to go,' I replied.

'Is that all?'

I can't think of anything else to say, especially to him.

I thought of the soft sweet smell of Susan, her gentle hair and warm arms and her wonderful kindness. A great wave of sadness washed over me, but the last person in the whole world I wanted to talk to about it was the Welsh bastard. I felt terrible for what I had put her through.

I had such a melancholy loneliness and it was too precious to share with that smug Welsh idiot. It all came back, not the bad times but the early days that seemed a lifetime away, days like a childhood, that were lost forever and nothing could ever really bring back. I could see the little attic flat where life had been so sweet and simple and I wondered what went wrong.

'I mean, it was all so simple,' I said. 'How on earth could it have all gone wrong?'

'You tell me.'

Was that all he could fucking say, or could he just not be bothered?

'You look back at all the things you did and it's like you were in a TV play,' I said. 'Is it like that for everyone?'

The doctor said nothing. He sat pink-eyed on the other side of the desk as if I was part of a faraway illusion. Outside, autumn was fading and the lunatics, turned out by the nurses, were floating around in the late sunshine.

'Is it all going to become a dream?' I continued. 'Even what's happening now? Is that what's happening to all that lot out there wandering through the gardens? Have they lost all reality?'

The doctor began biting the skin round his nails. He looked at his watch. My fifteen minutes of being mended was almost up, but he didn't say anything.

'You look at things and you don't seem to see how they are. You see them, you see what they're doing. You hear what they're saying. You know the meaning of every word, but it doesn't mean anything. It isn't real. It's like watching a foreign film. Is that how it is for everybody?'

The doctor came into focus and I heard him say, 'I don't know. How can I know how it is for everybody?'

God, I hated the Welsh.

'But is it like that for other people?'

'Who?'

'All them out there. All the madmen in the garden,' I said.

'Who can say?'

'But...'

'I can't speak for them.'

'But you're the doctor, you're supposed to know about these things.'

'All I can say,' he said, 'is that while you're here, you're one of them.'

The sky grew flat and dark grey. The last leaves died and fell in piles until the trees were lifeless skeletons. Walking through the buried grass was walking on death. The air fell still as if it too had died and the rain came straight down like lace curtains.

I sat in the Quiet Room looking out into the overcast gloom. It was midday but it felt like night. The rain, soundless itself through the thick lunatic-proof glass, soaked up the other sounds from the outside world. Traffic that usually rumbled and hummed all day on the other side of the fence was drowned out. It seemed for a few minutes as if the whole world had died.

My depression lost the frantic edge that it had outside and developed into something deeper and more fundamental like it was adjusting itself to fit me permanently. With my mind blurred by massive doses of tranquillisers, the depression grew frighteningly comfortable and familiar like an old friend. It held me like a gentle lover, but it held me closer than any person ever had and wrapped me up in an ever-tightening grip.

I never learnt to swim at school, the only one out of a class of thirty. This lapse hadn't been due to any rebellion or personal feelings against my teachers. The reason I never learnt was because of a deep unfounded terror. There had been three or four of us boys cowering at the shallow end, but one by one the others had been coaxed into deeper water, leaving me on my own to walk

slowly, as if through treacle, backwards and forwards across the pool, moving my arms in the pretence of the breaststroke but always keeping my feet firmly on the ground.

I had desperately wanted to learn to swim.

I went alone after school and splashed about while children less than half my age threw themselves off the highest diving board. I told myself that away from the pressure of my friends I would learn. It was like riding a bicycle. You only had to do it once and then you could always do it, but I knew that no matter how often I went I would never learn and I didn't until I was thirty-five years old.

Now the ground had slipped away from beneath me and I was drowning. This time there was no shallow end to run to, no teacher to throw me a rope or jump in and save me. Every time the tips of my toes touched something solid it slipped away at a frightful angle into bottomless depths that went down into cold darkness.

It wasn't any consolation to know there were others like me and undoubtedly others worse than me who would end up killing themselves. I didn't care if there were a million other souls in torment, it didn't make mine any better.

There were people in Springfield who had passed where I was years before. They were led along by others, shuffle, shuffle in cheap government slippers, moving wallpaper. Silent or silenced, the shuffle, shuffle the only noise, broken here and there with 'Come on, Doris, it's shepherd's pie today.'

Shuffle, shuffle.

'We like shepherd's pie, Doris, don't we?'

Shuffle, shuffle.

Yes, yes, we all like shepherd's pie, don't we?

Oh God, we're all eating the same food.

Down the middle of the corridors, in the short-stay lane, everyone else hurried by to get the best tables, to get the orange squash before it ran out and there was only tap water left, or to get the chairs by the windows or the chairs by the TV or the new pencils or use the razor before nine other people or just find the quietest place out in the grounds.

DEADLY TOXINS FOR
FUN AND PLEASURE

As time has gone by, things that everyone thought were harmless have turned out to be really good at killing you or at least making you very ill. Marie Curie used to handle uranium a lot and there was a time when radioactivity was actually thought to be good for you. You could even buy radioactive underwear.

By the time I was born everyone knew radioactivity was A BAD THING.

But we didn't know that mercury was also A BAD THING and I can remember spending hours playing with the mercury out of broken thermometers. I kept some in a matchbox.

I suspect that future generations will realise that a very high percentage of the crap in fast food is called 'fast' because that's the speed at which it buggers you up.

As for Vegemite and Marmite and currants, raisins and sultanas, I've known since I was a tiny little boy that they are really evil and bad for you.

THE WHOLE TRUTH AND NOTHING BUT THE TRUTH AND THE GREATEST NOVEL EVER WRITTEN

While I was in Springfield Hospital I became an experiment.

I was put in a quiet room with a tape-recorder. A doctor stuck a needle in the back of my hand and injected two big syringes full of chemicals into me. I'm not sure what they all were, but one of them was the so-called 'truth drug' Sodium Pentothal. There was other stuff too, including something that kept me hyperactive and wide awake for at least two days.

They then gave me a piece of paper with a list of trigger words written on it like – mother, father, childhood, sex, etc., turned on the tape recorder and left me to talk.

So I talked.

And talked…

And talked…

And every hour someone came in put a fresh reel of tape on the recorder.

Truth drug – that's crap, I thought, but it wasn't. I would come to something embarrassing, tell a lie, start giggling and say, 'Well actually, what really happened was…' and then tell the truth.

After three hours, I decided I needed to write a book. It was going to be the greatest book that anyone had ever written. When they came with the next reel of tape I asked them if I could have lots of pens and paper. So when they brought my lunch and the fifth reel, they brought me writing stuff.

I wrote an entire fantastic, incredible, total work of genius novel that I was absolutely certain would make me one of the greatest authors ever. The fact that I had never written a thing before and had been completely crap at English in school was swept away by my phenomenal inspiration.

So I ate my lunch, stopped talking for a bit and wrote what was destined to be one the ten greatest works of literature ever.

After about an hour I had covered both sides of over two hundred sheets of paper without pausing for a second and finished.

So I switched the recorder back on and did some more lying, giggling and telling the truth and filled another reel of tape.

I had produced six hours of almost non-stop talk plus an epic work of literature.

The next day, still several feet above the ground with the drugs I'd been given, I sat down to read my masterwork. I had over two hundred sheets of one hundred per cent illegible scribble. I had written everything at such a phenomenal speed that there wasn't one single legible word, not even a simple word like 'the'. I did have a really sore wrist though.

Naturally I was a bit upset that the world was to be denied my amazing book, a book that that I couldn't remember one single detail of, not even the title.

As for my six hours of tape, I asked, but I was never allowed to hear any of it, though I did hear a few nurses talking to each other about it in muttered tones that included a lot of 'wow's, 'oh, the poor thing's and the occasional 'I don't believe it.'

CT | He followed the grass into the shadows and made a small hotel | 1993

1962 – THE MIRRORBALL
OF THE GODS

'In the great ballroom that is life, we are all mere
reflections in the mirrorball of the Gods.'
Louis d'Appolières – Patagonian philosopher 1827–1913

Like so many people in Springfield, the mirrorball had seen better days. For one or two people, which I hoped included me, the better days were yet to come. Without that dream, suicide could become an obvious path.

The shiny globe turned for two hours every week, one hour on Tuesdays and the other on Thursdays from three till four. That was when Springfield danced officially, though in mental hospitals all over the world there's always somebody dancing somewhere.

In Springfield, twenty people went dancing – the room too small for more, though I never saw anyone turned away. They were all very old and most had to be led there by nurses. A few remembered and would be waiting by the door of the little one-room-and-a-lavatory building that stood on its own out in the hospital grounds surrounded by tidy grass. If you spent time out in the grounds, you knew about the dancing because you could hear the music drifting across the field.

So one week I followed them inside and waited for the music to begin.

At first nothing happened and then slowly, the mirrorball began to move. For a while it ran smoothly and then for no reason, it gave a few epileptic shudders and dropped a couple of its tiny mirrors that caught the light like snowflakes as they fell to the ground. Then it came to a complete halt for a bit, like it was deciding what to do next, before resuming its slow rotation. I imagined a tiny person inside the mirrorball, pedalling it like a bicycle, an old goblin who smoked cigarettes, which would explain the burning smell, and who sometimes fell asleep. In Springfield, many things had tiny people living inside them, including a lot of the patients.

Once upon a time, there had been a spotlight in each corner of the room that shone on the mirrorball, but when I was there, three of the spotlights had stopped working and no one had replaced them.

I really liked the mirrorball, not for its eccentric behaviour or its beautiful sparkles that look like a reflection of lost happiness, but simply for the fact that it was there at all. Where had it come from and why? It had obviously once been in a grand ballroom somewhere. It was far too big for the tiny bedroom-sized building it now lived in. Had there been a meeting where it had actually been discussed, item forty-six between the buckles that kept breaking on the straight-jackets and the problem with George with the Grey Balls who wouldn't stop taking his clothes off every time the sun came out? It was impossible to imagine the hospital board being light-hearted enough to sanction the purchase of a mirrorball, not unless Freud or Jung had recommended their use in some sort of therapy, which in the world of psychiatry is completely possible. I think it must have been left to the hospital in a rich eccentric person's will, so that even if the doctors didn't want it there, they had to in order to get a bequest.

Everything we did, no matter how small, got written down in a book. This wasn't a paranoid fantasy. I saw the books once, rows of them on shelves in an office. I don't think we were supposed to know about the books, but I actually looked inside one once when the doctor was called out in a rush when Gerald with the Twitch Who Never Spoke went down to Tooting Bec underground station and threw himself under a train.

Of course none of the dancers noticed the mirrorball's erratic behaviour so they missed the irony of its strange performance mimicking theirs. Most of the dancers didn't notice anything on this planet. They lived where the grass was pink and the sky was covered with little flowers and marshmallows. They'd gone to live there when this planet became too much to take any more. Some of them went there long before I was born. Some went slowly and others in a few days and there they were facing each other in pairs, holding hands and walking in slow unreliable circles around the floor while the music played. Moving statues with far away eyes. Some were aware there was another person in front of them, but most would have been just as happy dancing with a shopping trolley.

They had used up their as-good-as-it-gets bits long ago and the two hours' dancing every week was as good as it was ever going to be for the rest of their lives.

The detail of the music was not important. Fast, slow, Mozart, rock and roll, it was all the same, because the dancers never changed their steps. The music was just a switch that started them moving.

Music = move.

No music = stand still.

They didn't hear the music itself because they were all listening to their memories. Sometimes there was an uncanny moment when all twenty of them seemed to synchronise their movements and sway from left to right as they went clockwise round the room, like an eerie ballet or a field of grass swaying in the wind, all part of one large creature, one breath, one thought, a supernatural symbiosis. This didn't happen very often but when it did, an amazing feeling of peace filled the room.

I was about fifty years too young to dance and besides, I had no one to dance with.

And then, the third time I went, I met Edna.

She was fifty years too young too with short blonde hair and a beautiful face, bright blue eyes and a slim perfect body. I'd never seen her before. The staff didn't all wear uniforms so I assumed that's what she was, but she was a patient, same as me.

She came over and we swapped names and then she said, 'Do you want to go somewhere and fuck?'

I very, very much wanted to do exactly that, so we walked to the far side of the field, hid in the bushes and did, and someone watching from a distant window wrote it down in the book.

We were both allowed out during the day so we went on the bus to Richmond Park and walked across the open grass past the deer and lay down out of sight and fucked.

We went on the underground to Kew Gardens and fucked among trees and bushes from all over the world. We wanted to in one of the tropical hot houses, but they were full of old ladies with easels and watercolours.

One weekend we ran away to Brighton, to a cheap room four blocks back from the sea, with wallpaper older than our parents and plumbing that shuddered more than we did and a window that looked out at a bare wall, and for the first time we saw each other naked, naked from head to toe. We were so beautiful. We were little children again, open and shameless, sleeping in each other like incestuous siblings, and on Saturday night when all the world was asleep and the late drunks had collapsed in the bus shelters, we went down to the beach and made love on the rolling shingle. The cold night air staggered up the beach from the English Channel, so we went back to our bed.

It's still the greatest escape, sex. To fuck was to forget and it was the closest we could be to each other, parts of one body inside the other, glued together by loneliness. I think our hearts were too numb for love then, yet it was a kind of love with no conditions, no demands, no fight for control and that was more than millions of people had. And I never saw a single reason for the beautiful Edna, with her short blonde hair and blue eyes so full of excitement and tomorrow, to be inside an asylum. It's an unwritten rule in hospitals that you never ask anyone why they're there. It's obvious with a lot of people, but Edna was so wonderfully normal.

But she was on Largactyl, which I think in 1962 meant only one thing. Schizophrenia.

There should have been a voice inside my head, telling me I had a wife and daughter, but it wasn't there. I had really truly loved Susan and thought we would be together for ever, but it had got broken. I was in no state to work out why it had all gone wrong. There had been no reason for it to do so, but it had and all I knew was that when things got broken there was usually no way of ever putting them back together again.

It's like when your dog/cat dies. There are two things you can do. One is grieve and mourn and wait until the pain passes which could be months until one day you find yourself thinking you might be ready for a new dog/cat. Some imagined guilt tells you that no new pet could ever be the same as the old one, but you think you might grow to love the new dog/cat as much, but in a sort of different way which will make it all right.

The second way is to go straight out and find a new dog/cat/person to love. Waiting will not bring your old dog/cat/person back and not waiting does not mean you loved them any less than if you had waited for months. It is simply time to move on and find one that you hope will last forever.

I always take the second path and if people think it's selfish and shallow that's their problem. I have a terrible need for as little emptiness in my life as possible. Love makes all the bad stuff go away. It's a survival technique. I'm not sure if it works, but I think it's the only one I've got apart from escaping to the inside of my head.

So when I met Edna it was wonderful like it had been when I had first met Sue, and like I had with Sue, I wanted Edna to last forever.

In a place where all the values were upside down, life and death weren't big deals and I had a close experience of it one lunchtime when five of us, safe patients, went down the road from the hospital to the pub. We sat in the bar

like real people, a pint each, a cigarette each and a dirty joke each. Everyone else in the pub knew where we were from but no one dared say anything. The mad are unpredictable. No one knew what we might do, so they left us alone.

'I won't be a minute,' said a bald man from my ward, 'I'm just going to throw myself under a bus.'

And he did.

And someone else said, 'So who's going to have his beer?'

And on the jukebox Little Jimmy Dickens was singing *May the Bird of Paradise Fly Up Your Nose.*

The police arrived. An ambulance came and took the body away. Someone from the hospital arrived and escorted us back and after that we weren't allowed to go to the pub for two weeks.

That was it.

Life went on, or not.

It was only later that night, as I was dropping off to sleep, that it hit me just how indifferent we'd all been. If the dead man, who may have left a family overwhelmed with grief, had said, *'I won't be a minute, I'm just going to get a packet of fags,'* we would have reacted in exactly the same way and it hadn't just been me. All of us had been equally unconcerned. I suppose it was an automatic self-protection system, another survival technique that kicks in when you're in a place like Springfield.

Being in a mental hospital with depression goes through several stages. At first I didn't know where I was. Then I realised, but I didn't care, and then it became frightening. Everyone has heard about people going into loony bins and never being seen again. Then the routine kicked in and it wasn't scary any more because I knew that I could just leave whenever I wanted to unless they sectioned me.

Up to that point, it was all right. Once the pain eased a bit, which was inevitable with all responsibilities lifted from your shoulders, it was almost like being on holiday or back in your childhood in those days when you were wrapped up safe from the world in a box of cotton wool.

It was the next bit that became dangerous.

Life became comfortable. You never had to go out into the cold or the rain or do the washing-up or the cooking or shopping or laundry, pay the rent or feed the dog or ever think about anyone else's feelings. All you had to do was get up in the morning, eat at the right times, swallow your pills, keep quiet and go to bed at night.

It got very, very easy especially when there was someone to have sex with and a TV to watch and a snooker table in the ward, which there always was.

Then the really bad bit happens. You start adopting the mannerisms of the mad. Strange little affectations and routines creep into your daily life. I imagined the day when I too would close my hands, would open my hands, would mutter under my breath and tap my forehead before every sip of tea. I could see myself jumping sideways through open doors to avoid the shadows and turning in circles, like a dog getting ready to sleep, before sitting in my chair.

I was on the verge of becoming institutionalised and I knew it was time to go.

But it was so hard and of course I was no closer, not even a few millimetres, to knowing how or why I had got so broken. No one talked about that. You were just left to your own devices to wait for the tide to go out.

It was safe and comfortable and there was Edna. Springfield had become home. The water was calm in there and outside there were storms waiting, but I knew I had to go before it was too late. I had to turn the outside back into the real world again and Springfield back into the place where crazy people went. And I had to stop being a crazy person.

After three months in Springfield, by which time I'd managed to get a room of my own, I got into trouble for covering its walls in collages. The nurses and patients loved them because they made them laugh, but the hospital manager had brought a tour of worthy bodies around and they hadn't loved them. I suppose if they had, it would have told me they weren't very good – the collages that is, not the administrators.

I was ordered to take them all down.

Fuck off.

I phoned Aunt Pam, and Uncle Ted came with my cousin Stephen and rescued me. I wanted to leave without the authorities knowing I'd gone. They wouldn't have cared, but I just wanted to make it a little bit embarrassing for them when they discovered I hadn't been at dinner or breakfast and hadn't told anyone. I imagined them poking about in the piles of leaves in case I was there, cold and dead – though I suppose if I had been, it would have been swept under the carpet along with the quietly assisted unloved and forgotten ancients who died peacefully in their sleep.

I packed my bag and slipped it to Ted who took it out to his car parked in the street outside and he and Stephen waited while I ran round everywhere trying to find Edna to say goodbye, but I couldn't find her.

There should be photos of Edna here, but I never had a single one. Cameras and all that stuff are not things you think about when you are deep in depression, especially as this was long before digital cameras and mobile phones so you had to buy a film and then take it to the chemist to get developed and printed. I don't ever remember seeing a single looney, in any of the three hospitals I was in, with a camera. Nor did I have a camera later on when I lived in Bristol. For a few years I could shut my eyes and still see Edna, but that faded away a long, long time ago and all I've got now are the words that describe her — short blonde hair, beautiful bright blue eyes, pale skin and a slim perfect body. I wonder if I saw a photograph now whether I'd recognise her. I'm sure I would.

1963 – OVER SOME DIFFERENT AND COMPLETELY FLAT HILLS AND...

I woke up one morning in my bedroom at my parent's flat with a perfect clear future in my head. Suicide. There was no melodrama to it. It just seemed, above all else, the most sensible thing to do. One day, after years riddled with recurring depression, I would have grown old and then I would die. Cutting out all the agony in between seemed such a clear-headed obvious solution.

So I walked round to the tiny flat where Susan and Charlotte were living. I went, not to say goodbye because I hadn't thought of that. I just wanted to see my wife and child one last time. I had no intention of telling Sue what I was going to do.

I'm sorry, so sorry. I never wanted to hurt you. I never wanted to hurt anyone, not even myself or the cat who fell off the roof.

We drank tea and while Sue was putting Charlotte to bed for a nap, I swallowed the pills. I said goodbye and walked home to my parents' flat. It was only five minutes away.

Sleep was coming and soon I'd be sleeping in my bed.

I can't remember walking home, and then it was dark and my throat felt like it had been sandpapered.

There were noises and smells I didn't know and I didn't want to open my eyes, but something wasn't right. I could hear voices, voices I didn't know. They weren't talking to me and they were just a little too far away to make out what they were saying.

I don't want to be awake. I just want to, I just want to...

Oh God, I was sitting in Sue's kitchen. I'd the swallowed the pills and I was going home.

And now I should be dead.

Please, please, let me be dead.

But I knew I wasn't.

I was sure your throat wouldn't hurt if you were dead and you wouldn't be able to smell disinfectant.

I'm going to open my eyes now. I'm not dead. I'm in hospital. There are nurses and beds with other people in. There's a tube coming out of my arm.

Oh fuck, fuck, fuck, why didn't it work?

'So how are we feeling now, then?' a voice said.

It was a Jamaican nurse. She came and sat on my bed.

'You're lucky someone found you,' she said.

No I'm not. It was supposed to work.

'No,' is all I could say.

'Sure you are, darlin',' she said. 'You're too young to die.'

'No.'

'You sleep now,' she said and I closed my eyes and drifted off into semi-consciousness. Maybe if I could go back to sleep again there might be enough of the pills left inside me to finish the job.

I was so angry it hadn't worked. If only I'd just gone into my bedroom and taken the pills there, instead taking them before I left Sue's, it would all be over now.

'It won't work,' a loud voice muttered close to my face.

The crazy Welsh psychiatrist from Springfield was sitting on a chair by my bed.

'It won't work, you know,' he said.

'What?'

'We're not taking you back,' he said. 'You don't fool me.'

'What do you mean?'

'People who really want to kill themselves always succeed,' he said.

'I didn't,' I said.

'You didn't mean to. You just want to get back into the hospital,' he said.

'Fuck off.'

'That's it,' he laughed.

The next day they sent me home. I wasn't glad it hadn't worked. I had honestly wanted it to.

But I didn't try again.

'Here,' said my stepfather, stuffing £100 into my hand, 'go away.'

Which was exactly what I had been planning to do, but now I had funds to do it which was great.

I packed a holdall and went to Paddington Station. I looked up at the departure boards and wondered where to go.

Bristol.

Why?

I hadn't the faintest idea. I had never been there in my life and knew nothing about it, nor did I know anyone from there. As far as I knew I'd never

even met anyone who had been there, but then that applied to thousands of places, so why not?

There was a train leaving in ten minutes so I bought a ticket.

We raced through a flat and uneventful land. Drizzle turned to rain that streaked against the windows from a sky that was the standard British summer grey.

It would be good now, I thought, *if I could leave most of my thoughts behind in London because right now I'm feeling neutral.*

Except for Edna.

With every mile the train moved away from London, I missed her more and more.

There was a new life beckoning from a new town. I half-suspected that it would probably just be the same life in another place, but it was worth a try and I wanted Edna in it.

I wished I could have gone back to Spain and taken Edna with me, to the endless blue skies, but I couldn't afford it. Life always seemed so much simpler when the sun was shining all the time. But at least in Bristol I could get money and be cared for by the state until I got a job – and I wanted to get a job, to do the getting up each day and going to the same place and working for eight hours and going home again thing like I used to do. And I wanted Edna to be there too.

It was still raining when the train arrived in Bristol. It was four o'clock in the afternoon and dull like autumn, even though it was summer. It was the sort of weather designed to make you depressed – sombre wet streets with the air so thick you could almost drink it. That was Britain and her bloody awful weather. It created the British sense of misery that is part of all of us.

Even when the sun is shining, we're in love and have just eaten the best lunch we've ever had followed by fantastic sex, the British are still miserable because we know that, sooner rather than later, the blinds will be drawn across the sky, the rain will start again and the spirits will be dampened to the point of mildew.

Thank God humans aren't made of metal. We would have all disintegrated years ago.

But having spent hardly any time in a place of endless bright sunshine, England was where I felt most at home then, with an inherited need to complain about the weather and be constantly surprised when the sun shone for more than an hour. When it shone for three days in a row, it made the newspapers.

So in Bristol I wanted to start again as if what had gone before was just a practice and now I was ready to begin life properly. I'd made all the mistakes I needed to and now I could start over and get it right.

My parents, my friends and the places I grew up in were all left behind. I would have had new fingerprints and new teeth if I could, but instead I threw away my watch and my favourite shoes.

The train pulled into Bristol. I looked out and saw a station like any other with wide grey platforms and splashes of bright clothes as people hurried through their lives.

I picked up my bag and left the station and it was then, for the first time, that I felt a sudden wave of panic. Until I had touched Bristol with my feet I'd still been in London. Now I was a hundred miles from home, a hundred miles from the doctors and the hospital and the pills that had sort of kept me safe.

The panic only lasted a few minutes before the excitement of a new place and the overwhelming need to reject everything from the past took over again. And the panic, although natural, proved to be quite unnecessary.

I was outside the station in a place I'd never been to before. I found a taxi and told the driver I was looking for a room. We drove to a noticeboard outside a newsagents and I wrote down phone numbers.

The third one looked promising. She had a room, but when I met her, I didn't want it.

'I know where you're from,' she said. 'I've been there.'

I knew she had. I'd seen her. Not her exactly, but others like her, sixty-five years old, alone and drained by life, empty heart, picking invisible flies out of their soup, knitting clothes for the babies they never had, hiding in dreams they'd got from cheap novels. Alone everywhere except inside their own heads.

She told me she could see it in my eyes.

'You'll be all right here,' she said, Mrs Evans the crazy Welshwoman. I wondered if she was related to the crazy Welsh psychiatrist.

Home away from home or rather asylum away from asylum. It was the last thing I wanted, but I took the room. It would do for a start until I could find a job and move somewhere better.

It was OK. She kept herself to herself and didn't mind that I hadn't got a job to go to. She said she understood, but I didn't want her to understand. If a crazy lady like Mrs Evans understood me, what did that make me?

This week, I think I'll sleep, but first I'll write to Edna.

When I was nineteen, I pretty well stopped drawing and painting.
When I was forty-two I started again. This was the first picture I drew – Max's Café.

1963 – SO CLOSE TO PERFECT

As I saw Edna coming through the barrier I felt suddenly shy. She looked so beautiful, her short gold hair and her large eyes that lit up when she saw me. I couldn't believe that she'd come all this way just to be with me. I felt so privileged that she had put her future in my hands. She was shy too and we kissed like strangers, then stood in silence with our arms around each other.

It seemed like a hundred years since we'd been together in Springfield, but it had only been only been a month.

'Hello,' she said and so did I.

Neither of us could think of anything else to say.

I had a job by then – designing things to put cigars in on pub counters for a small plastics factory that then manufactured them for a huge tobacco company. And I'd left the crazy Welsh lady's house. It would have been a really bad place to have taken Edna, too much crazy stuff and the whole place felt kind of dirty. I'd moved to a nicer part of town, to a beautiful big room with a high ceiling. Its large windows looked out onto the overgrown garden of a tall house in a quiet old Victorian street.

The landlord lived in another town and the other tenants were so quiet and invisible that in all the time I lived there I never saw a single one of them. Their very existence was only revealed by the smell of cooking that drifted through the hall each evening. The whole house was as still as the hours of early morning, as if all the other tenants were ghosts or at least moved around in soft slippers and never spoke to one another.

The hospital seemed so distant then, all gone away like a strange dream, so far away that it felt as if it had happened to other people not us.

Life became neat and tidy once more. Edna was so beautiful and funny and gentle. We curled up in our nest, safe and self-contained, two lost children hiding from our torments and when we made love, it felt so full of love.

There were no problems in our world.

They were all outside in the other world. If only we never had to go out into it. We woke up each morning and made love before I went to work. And each evening as soon as I got home we made love again. Sometimes I raced home at lunchtime just to be with her for ten breathless minutes.

And I think it was love we were making then, not just sex. It was happy, smiling, laughing, frightened, innocent love. Full of lust and nuzzled sweat but full, too, of the tenderness of love that terrifies the heart.

Edna was the only woman apart from Gabrielle O'Reilly who ever stood naked before me without the slightest hint of reserve. All the others in between had held a shyness that I too had.

Edna came to me with her blue eyes and her heart and every little thing wide open. Later, I wondered if it was from a shameless childhood or the shadows of madness.

Not that it mattered then, it was so beautiful that the memory of it still makes me tremble. I sat on the bed and Edna stood naked in front of me. She walked over to me without a word, climbed up onto the bed and pulled my face into her thighs. It was so exciting. I fell backwards and she came down over me until I could hardly breathe. She clutched my head and held it tight until she came.

One of the house ghosts moved quietly down the hall five feet from where we were as I begged my brain to let me remember that moment for ever, to hold the taste and smell of her on my face.

If we could've kept every detail of that moment alive, I knew we would never be mad again. She rocked and moaned softly and as her orgasm shook her she began to cry. The tears rolled down her face onto my forehead, the warm rain of her sad life, locked up in her head, crying out for love.

She knelt completely still for a long time. Out in the garden two cats began to fight with frantic screams and out in the street the world carried on as if nothing had happened.

The perfection of the moment made all the other moments seem worse than ever. For several months we lived this perfect happiness. While I was at work Edna cooked and washed and mended and slept.

On Fridays we went dancing. On Saturdays we went shopping and on Sunday mornings we went to the pub where people began to nod and say hello. If we missed a week they even said, 'Didn't see you last Sunday.'

We saved enough money to go to Spain and lie in the sun and make love on the beach. We talked and planned about going as soon as the winter in Bristol got really cold.

I hadn't taken any pills for months. I'd flushed my Librium and Sodium Amytal down the toilet. Edna still took her Largactyl every day. After all this

time we still never talked about our illnesses. It was taboo. Edna seemed so normal that I couldn't imagine there was anything seriously wrong with her.

But then when life is good, it's so often too good to last.

I came home from work one day and Edna was asleep in bed. It wasn't unusual so I climbed in beside her, but she didn't move. I tried to wake her but, I couldn't. Then I saw the empty pill bottle by the bed.

I was suddenly so scared.

Then I saw the note.

It's OK, I'm really tired and I need to sleep, it said. *Just leave me.*

I wanted to believe it.

I so, so wanted to believe it.

But, but I couldn't.

I was really scared.

Edna seemed to be hardly breathing. I tried to shake her awake, but she was so far away I knew she wasn't just sleeping.

I rang 999 and they arrived five minutes later and took her away.

They didn't tell me which hospital and I forget to ask.

When I found the right one and went to see her, she screamed at me.

'You fucking bastard. Didn't you see my note? I said I just wanted to sleep.'

I told her I was frightened, but whatever I said she screamed more until the nurse made me leave.

Outside in the corridor I saw the doctor.

'Did she take enough pills to kill herself?' I asked him.

'Who are you?' he said.

'We live together.'

'Are you married?'

'No, but we've been living together for ages.'

'Well I'm afraid I can't tell you,' he said, fucking smug superior bastard.

I told him she's an ex-mental patient. I told him we'd been together for a long time but nothing would make him change his mind.

The bastard asked someone to escort me out. If only I'd known, I could have lied and said we were married.

Back in our room, I sat in despair. It had all collapsed again and I wanted to run. If I stayed I'd fall to pieces, but there wasn't really anywhere to go.

Her clothes were everywhere. I held them to my face and I could smell her and although my heart was breaking I still couldn't remember how to cry.

Oh Edna, I wish I knew why you did it. You broke my heart, just when all the bits were getting stuck back together again. And what of your heart, was it broken too? Are we both like bits of pottery, once broken impossible to mend?

The next week a social worker came and collected her stuff and I never saw Edna again. I stayed in our room and became twenty-one and no matter how I tried, I could never find out whether she meant to kill herself and if she had meant to did she try it again until she succeeded? That's what I thought was the most likely thing. A few years later, it occurred to me that she might have been pregnant. We'd had lots of sex and never taken any precautions. So if she'd been pregnant, had she had an abortion or do we have a child somewhere? Now, of course, we have both reached an age where she could have died without suicide.

All I know is that of all the people there have been in my life, Edna was the one whose memory came back the most often.

2015 – I tried to find Edna on ancestry.com and the only name that seemed to fit died when she was 27. She was found dead on an island in the Thames from an overdose of barbiturates. She must have crossed the footbridge looking for a quiet place to die. I can't stop thinking about how unutterably sad and lonely she must have been.

I drew this picture years before I knew any of this.

I hope it wasn't her, but I am sure it must be. How can there be any kind of God when schizophrenia and suicide could happen to such a beautiful, innocent and wonderful person?

1963 TO 1966 – DIVORCES – PART 1

My bedsit was the nearest to the front door so if the bell rang, which it hardly ever did, I usually answered it.

There was a small grey man there in a raincoat and he was holding a letter.

'Colin Thompson?' he said.

'Yes.'

'This is for you,' he said offering me the letter, which of course I took.

'What is it?' I said, after he had let go of it, but he had shot out of the gate and was running off down the road.

I hadn't the faintest idea what was going on.

It was a petition for a divorce.

Sue and I had talked about divorce. There didn't seem any point in not getting one. She was living with Marshall and I was living in fantasia or somewhere with someone else or not. We agreed that I was going to divorce her because I would be twenty-one first and she had nearly a year to wait and would have had to get her parents to sign forms. But by then, she had become twenty-one and there I was with a piece of paper saying that she was going to divorce me. Her solicitor had told her that was the best thing to do.

Neither of us had any money so we had both applied for and been granted Legal Aid, which was designed to pay our costs. So Sue and I agreed to cross-petition, which meant we would divorce each other.

I named Marshall as Sue's partner in adultery. Sue named quite a lot of people,* several of whom had been friends of hers, as mine.

Then we both forgot about it for the next couple of years.

---

* *The authorities thought there were too many names on my list so they took away my Legal Aid on 'moral grounds'. Of course, this meant my appointed solicitor dropped me instantly, and quite right too.*

How To Live Forever

COLIN THOMPSON

1963 – AFTER EDNA

After Edna it was difficult. I had no room inside my head for lots of things, certainly not for any complications.

I went to work each day. I walked through the plastics factory to the studio that first week after she had gone and nodded hello to everyone, but I couldn't talk, not even to the girls who were smiling at me. London girls didn't smile like that. They all lived on pedestals and I always forgot to take a box to stand on, but Bristol girls stopped you and smiled and asked questions in their lovely soft Bristol voices.

One of the factory girls told her friend to ask me if I'd like to take her out and, without being sure which one she was, I said OK. It would be Saturday night before I'd find out.

Lucy was blonde and pretty and the biggest girl I'd ever been out with. She wasn't fat, more voluptuous all over like the Venuses the old masters had painted and she was unlike any girl I'd known before. Inside her big body was a big heart with nothing but simple loving thoughts.

If someone had sat down and written a prescription for what I needed after Edna, it probably would have been Lucy. Lucy didn't want to talk about life and all its problems. She knew there weren't any. Lucy didn't want to talk about anything really. She just wanted to cuddle me and pull my face into her enormous breasts and make love.

Sometimes, when you let it be, life can be so simple. Through the coldest winter for nearly twenty years, while the ice lay uncleared on the roads for weeks, big soft Lucy wrapped her large warm body all round me.

It was just what I needed to help Edna's memories sink deeper and deeper into my subconscious.

Of course, it couldn't last.

Lucy started speaking.

'Talk to me,' she said. 'You never talk to me.'

'What about?'

We didn't have anything in common apart from the sex and there was nothing to say about that. We just did it.

'I don't know,' she said. 'Just talk to me about something.'

'Like what?' I said. 'I don't know what to say.'

'I don't know. Anything,' she said.

There were tears coming into her eyes and I really didn't know what to say.

'Tell me about when you were little.'

'But when I tried to talk to you before,' I said, 'you know, at first, you just wanted to go to bed and fuck. You didn't want to talk.'

'That was then,' Lucy said. 'It's different now.'

'Oh God, you're pregnant.'

'No, I'm not,' she said, 'but I wouldn't mind.'

She leant on one elbow looking down at me and said softly, 'I'm in love and I want to know things about you.'

There was nothing I could say. I couldn't say, 'I love you, too,' because as soon at the word love came into my head, there was Edna back again.

'It's all right,' I said, pulling Lucy's head onto my shoulder.

Later as I waited with her at the bus stop she said nothing and I knew it was over.

'You are too shallow to drown in,' she said.
I looked in my heart and my head.
The words that I wanted were missing,
So I led her by hand to the bed.
'You are too shallow to drown in,' she said.
I sat there thinking deep thoughts.
I longed for her arms but said nothing.
She cried and went out for a walk.
In the darkness down by the river
She stood throwing dreams at the moon.
'He is too shallow to drown in,' she said
And then went back to the room.
And the love in our hearts unable to fly
Crept away unseen and unsaid.
And the tears in our thoughts unable to cry
Drowned the dreams we had in our heads.
'You are too shallow to drown in,' she said.
I sat there unable to speak.
When at last I found the right words,
She'd been gone for nearly a week.

The next week, Lucy wasn't at work and work itself fell to bits. The boss was a dreadful man – five foot two of anger. He walked round the factory screaming obscenities at the workers.

It was a miracle no one thumped him. He didn't talk to the three of us in the studio like that, but one day he called me into his office to tell me that I had to go to work in a suit, not an old leather jacket and jeans.

'We have an image to project to our clients,' he explained.

I'll give you a fucking image, I thought and the next day wore my really old oil-paint splattered jeans and a sweater with an unravelling sleeve.

I was sent for and he went red and began to swear at me and I was so happy that he was only five foot two.

Bristol had gone cold. I couldn't get Edna out of my head and all the anger I'd been collecting since she nearly died was just what I needed to grab the swearing bastard by his shoulders and threaten to kill him.

Fifteen minutes later I left with one month's wages, one month's holiday pay and one month's 'bonus' all in cash. I drove my Vespa down to the finance company who I'd got slightly behind on my payments with and drove it carefully into one of those wide glass revolving doors where it got very stuck. I switched it off, took the lift up to their offices on the seventh floor and gave them the keys.

'It's downstairs,' I said, took the lift back down to reception, where two men were trying to remove the scooter from the revolving doors, went out of the side door and walked home.

Bristol had too many thoughts of Edna, so I packed my clothes, wrote *'Bye bye'* in the rent book and got the train back to London with a pair of her knickers in my pocket.

And all I'd ever wanted was to be in love forever.

I expect that's all most people want and I imagine that most of us manage it from time to time. How long and how often the forever is varies. Those are the bits we have no control over and I suppose not knowing just makes it all the more exciting when it happens, and, of course, you can have more than one forever.

SPOTS BEFORE, AFTER & BEHIND THE EYES

Until I was about eleven years old I was attacked by bananas. Every time I ate them I came out in spots, not just one or two, but global spots from head to toe covering every square inch of me. I can't remember how long the spots lasted or if my mother did anything to make them go away or even how much they itched. I think I was banana tested at regular intervals until one day nothing happened and from then on I could eat them whenever I liked, which wasn't very often. My youngest daughter Alice had the same thing and hers went away too at about the same age. I must ask her if either of her sons have it, but I think if they did she probably would have told me.

Years later when I was living in the Isle of Lewis, I got the same global spots, but without the aid of bananas. It always happened when I was asleep at night and it would wake me up with crazy itching as they crept up from my feet until they had covered me all over. I would sit up in bed and after about an hour they would gradually fade away. I think it happened about six times and I never found out what set it off.

I think now I've passed seventy, I must have finally finished puberty because it hasn't happened for a very long time.

LIVES OF QUIET DESPERATION*

The thought of going out there frightened me.

'You can go home for the weekend, if you like,' the doctor told me.

'No, it's all right.'

The second and third weekend it was the same, but the fourth time he said it, it wasn't a suggestion any more. I'd been in the hospital for nearly two months and in that time no one had come to see me, no mother, no Susan, no friends.

I didn't know why. Was someone telling them to stay away? I imagined my mother couldn't handle the shame of a child who was mentally ill. It would never have occurred to her in a million years that she might have had something to do with it. How on earth could she have?

For goodness sake, she was a fucking Christian.

'I've got nowhere to go,' I said.

'What about your parents?' the doctor suggested.

'No, I can't go there.'

The doctor made notes and made it clear that I had to go somewhere. He didn't care where just as long as it was outside.

That wasn't really the problem. I did have places to go, friends, relatives, but I didn't want to go out.

'Just for the weekend,' the doctor said, 'to see how you feel.'

I knew how I felt. In Springfield I felt safe. Out there I would feel bad, but it was no good saying that. It wasn't the right answer. It was no good telling him I was scared to go outside because that was where all the problems were.

So I went through the hospital gates, my heart racing ahead of me. I touched the outside world, tears nearly coming. Tears often nearly came but never did.

Legs weak.

Can I come back inside, please? I can't do it.

The road was another corridor and I clung to garden walls. I became a seventy-year-old woman in a lumpy cardigan shuffling through the streets to the station. I was out now in the big wide world but it felt claustrophobic, noise all around, clattering in my head like breaking china.

---

* *This wonderful phrase comes from Henry David Thoreau. I wish I had invented it.*

Panic pouring in

Have I got my pills? How much does the ticket cost and how far is it across the immense open space of the station?

As I waited for the train, I wanted to curl up and sleep, to wait until the world I used to know came back. On the train, I sat huddled at the end of the carriage, watching on auto-pilot.

Could everyone tell?

They could, couldn't they?

They were all looking at me, weren't they?

'Look children, there's a lunatic. Eat your vegetables or you'll end up like that.'

I've got news for you, lady. I ate all my carrots and look what it did for me.

Change here, cross platforms, not underground any more.

Help, everyone is staring.

Finally back in Ealing, turn right out of the station and I could be at my mother's in five minutes, but I turned left, ten minutes to the flat where Pete lived. He was the only friend I had who didn't live at home or wasn't away at university.

'Hi.'

Not much else to say really. So we got drunk and ate fish and chips. Beer and Librium don't mix. One bottle and I was far away.

I was OK then. It was all right in the flat, safe, not as safe as hospital, but safe, tidy walls, one on each side and one above the head and a solid floor, all visible boundaries, all safe. The Librium and beer knocked me out at nine o'clock. I woke two hours later to feel two arms holding me. It was Liz, wrapping me up like a baby.

Liz was a friend from Ealing Art School. We'd been in class together, always friends and never lovers. Pete had phoned her. I wondered why he hadn't phoned Susan. Maybe he had and she wouldn't come.

'How are you?' she said.

'Frightened,' I told her.

'Would you like me to come and visit you in hospital?' she asked.

'It's an awful long way. You don't have to.'

I turned towards her then, too shy to look into her eyes, and buried my face in her sweater. The fear of being outside had exhausted me and I wanted to sleep.

But then she said, 'Do you want to get under the covers?' and we undressed and she held me like a baby and I let the tears I'd held back since I was eleven pour down her skin.

It was so good to lie there in her arms. I knew we were not going to make love, but she was my friend and I needed that so much more.

'It's all right,' she said.

She knew more than I ever would. The tears ran and she stroked my back and held me to her breasts like a baby until I fell asleep.

Later, there were sudden noises in the darkness, drunk voices, crashing chairs, giggles.

'Oh fuck,' said Pete.

More giggles followed by the bed across the room creaking in frantic, fifty-second drunken sex.

'Oh shit, quick,' said a new voice.

The light came on and Pete was running naked round the room grabbing towels and a bucket. The owner of the voice, fat and red-faced with mascara flowing down her cheeks, sat up in bed and threw up, mostly into the bucket.

Pete was in love.

In our bed, Liz and I slid down under the covers as far as we could, while across the room Pete's future first wife fell back on the pillows and passed out. In the middle of the room, Pete, blissfully unaware of reality, said, 'Anyone like a cup of tea?'

Liz never came to Springfield. Back in the protection of the hospital walls, I felt safe again.

The second weekend out was easier. The walls kept still as I passed them. I got to Pete's place without incident and Liz came round again. We lay on the bed and she held me again. It was so good. Pete came in from work. We drank beer and Liz cooked and then we all went out to a dance. There was a blur in my eyes. It was the beer. I knew I wasn't supposed to drink with the pills.

There was music playing, some local band with Eric Clapton and Jack Bruce. We'd all heard them before, playing at The Ealing Club. It was loud and I was too out of it to dance so I sat at the side.

And then across the room I saw a face.

She was sitting down too. I knew lots of the people there. We went to the same art school, or The Ealing Club, but I'd never seen her before. She had long brown hair and a sad face of classical perfection. I was very tired but her face burnt into my heart as no other face had ever done before and I knew

that I would love her for the rest of my life, and even if I never saw her again, her face would live in my heart until the day I died.

I thought I would like to die then before the fleeting moment turned into pain, which it was bound to. It hurt so much already, that heavy band round the chest, my heart so full of bottomless desperation.

Love that carries a massive sadness that is too great to bear, but you know you will bear it because you have no choice.

I looked again and she'd gone. I told myself I was just drunk and it was all a stupid fantasy, but when I woke up the next morning, sober and alone back at Pete's, her face was the first thing I saw. It was in my head as bright as day and I didn't even know her name or anything about her.

Please don't let this be happening to me. I'm so full of pain already, I have no room for more.

The bell rang. It was Liz. We had coffee and I wanted to tell her about the woman with the sad face and the long brown hair, but it seemed unfair to talk to her about it. I knew we weren't lovers nor were we going to be, but she could see something was wrong so I told her.

'I don't believe it,' she said.

'What, love at first sight?' I said. 'It doesn't happen does it?'

'No, it's not that.'

'What is it then?'

'I know who she is and she rang me this morning because she saw me with you and she said the same thing about you.'

It was impossible, ridiculous, more than impossible and it couldn't be true and now more than forty years later it still seems ridiculous, but it really truly did happen.*

Her name was June. She was married. She had two children. She was twelve years older than me. And she felt the same as I did.

No, no, this is ridiculous.

'I'll take you to her,' Liz said, but I was too scared and shy to go.

What about her husband?

'They're separated.'

No, I can't.

'Look, it's all right,' Liz said. 'You have to go. This sort of thing only happens once in a lifetime. You have to go.'

---

* *Yes, I know – another French movie.*

I knew that how much it was hurting then was nothing to how much it was going to hurt. I knew that there was no way we would be allowed to have this. Things that perfect just aren't allowed to exist in Grown-Up World. I also knew that I had to go to her and we had to follow this unbearable love to its inevitable desperate conclusion.

My God, she only lived four streets away.

All that time she had been so close.

Then we were at her house and she was right there in front of me and the pain was even worse. I felt like I'd known her for a thousand years, like our souls had been part of one being forever and yet, I had never even heard her speak.

I was so desperately shy I couldn't say a word. Her two children were there and Liz took them round to the park to play on the swings.

And we were alone.

'I…' was about all I could say.

She came really close and took my hands and told me it was OK.

'You don't have to say anything,' she said, which was good because I couldn't.

We held each other and she said she felt the same as I did.

We lay on her bed and kissed soft kisses.

She was right.

There was nothing to say except, 'Oh God, I love you and it hurts so bad because I'm so scared.'

I was twenty years old. June was thirty-two. I was a manic-depressive on medication out from Springfield for the weekend. I already had one failed marriage and I hadn't even got to my twenty-first birthday.

I was the catch of the week.

She had one failed marriage and two children.

'Who would want to take me on?' she said.

I thought I should have said that bit. The blind were leading the blind, because who else would?

We wanted to make love, but we didn't because we knew we had forever and Liz would be back with the children soon. I wanted to spend every minute of my life with her, but the next morning I would have to go back to Springfield.

Except I felt ready to leave all that behind and be with June and her children. We would move to the country, get a cottage and live happily ever after.

Later that night, Liz had gone home and the children were asleep in bed and then we made love. We had candles and a lace scarf over the lamp and in their soft glow we undressed each other. June was as skinny as me. We were all ribs and hip-bones. She was taller than me and as we lay in each other's arms, she began to cry. There was no noise, just silent weeping for all the sad bad stuff in her life that should never have been. We made love and that was sad too. It was a sadness for the years we should have been together and hadn't been. I realised that when she was losing her virginity I was still a child just starting school.

Everything we had seemed so sad. I think we were exorcising our ghosts. When she came, it was in silent shallow waves that I could barely feel.

The best thing was waking up together in the morning. Her children were looking round the door, unsure of me. I wanted to pick them up and tell them everything was going to be all right, but I was too shy and I had to rush back to Springfield by 10 a.m.

Of course, as soon as it began, it was over. We both knew it was much too good to last, though I hadn't thought it would end quite so quickly.

I phoned her on Monday and it was wonderful.

On Tuesday someone told her husband and he had a fake suicide attempt, which was enough to put him in hospital and scare June into taking him back.

And that was it.

The greatest love of my life had lasted four days.

I never saw her again. The next weekend I stood in the street outside their flat, too scared to ring the bell, just hoping to see her face. Someone came out of the house and told me they'd left, gone down to her parents' farm in the country.

I often wondered how it would have been if we had stayed together. Would she have mended me? Would we have mended each other and lived happily ever after?

Maybe that's how it works.

You find someone who can give you so much happiness that it smothers the bad stuff. Maybe trying to find reasons and solutions is a pointless exercise. Maybe all you need is enough love to fill you to overflowing.

I walked back to Pete's place. He'd cheer me up, if only with Guinness.

'She's pregnant,' he said.

I didn't need to ask who. It was Jill, the big girl who had thrown up in the bucket. She was throwing up every morning then. She was at home with her parents and they were insisting on marriage.

'Maybe it's not yours,' I said.

He hadn't thought of that. He'd assumed she'd been as inexperienced as him, but everyone knew she'd slept with half the suburb.

'Come on,' I said. 'Let's run for it.'

After the pain of June, I was so ready to run, but I was tired too. Liz came and wrapped me in her arms at Pete's flat but before the weekend was over I crawled back to the security of Springfield.

Pete married Jill.

And I found out many years later, he used to beat her up. You don't expect people you know to do things like that. That sort of thing only happens in the papers. Bastard.

> # A MOTHER'S WIT AND WISDOM*
> *There was actually NO wit and very little wisdom
>
> Alice – 6, 'Granny, were there dinosaurs when you were a little girl?'
> Hannah – 8, 'Yes, Granny ran them all over.'

MY SECOND OLDEST FRIEND

My second oldest friend is called Raymund. We met at Hammersmith Art School – the one I went to after I got thrown out of Ealing Art School. Raymund, who was never Ray, and I had art in common, but then so did all of us – it was an art school. We became good friends and still are, though we haven't seen each other for a few years.

At one time we shared a room in a house of bedsitters in Golder's Green, a very Jewish suburb of London. The only other person in the house we got to know was Helen, an Australian girl who told us she had been a personal assistant to a famous American singer on her recent European tour. We didn't really believe her, but before we could talk about it, she was taken away to hospital for some big time serious surgery to have a kidney removed.

It was dark and raining and winter and there was a ring at the door. Standing out there in the rain was a large Negro lady and a man in a chauffeur's uniform. They'd come to see Helen.

It was Ella Fitzgerald.

And then Raymund inherited a small bag of money. It wasn't enough to doing anything grand like buying a house so Raymund decided we should go to Paris.

'And,' he said, 'we will travel in style. We will fly there.'

We got on a derelict coach in the middle of London and drove to an airport that was so close to the edge of the English Channel that the runway was probably underwater at high tide. The ancient Dakota creaked and complained and didn't so much take off as fall off the edge of England. Before we could fasten the seat belts that weren't there, we'd landed in France and climbed onto another derelict coach for the long drive into Paris.

We got a very cheap room in a very cheap pension off the Boulevard Saint Michel and went out and got seriously drunk and ate fish and chips just like we'd been doing in London, but now we were doing it in French. We slept in the double bed head to feet, which was good because during the night I threw up over Raymund's feet.

I tried to tell him the next morning just how awful it would have been if we'd both had our heads at the same end, but he didn't really appreciate it.

We did the art stuff, went to the galleries, sneered at the artists painting in the street, walked along the Seine (which looked remarkably like an English river, brown and dirty). We bought striped T-shirts, got drunk again, ate something that wasn't fish and chips, smoked some more French fags and went home.

In the few days we'd been in France, the company that had 'flown' us over had lost a wing off the plane, fortunately while crawling along the runway, not in the sky, and gone bankrupt, so we went home on the ferry, had more beer and more fish and chips and did not throw up on anyone's feet. The boat-train was slightly quicker than the plane had been.

Then we started scratching.

'Oh shit,' I said, 'they're moving.'

'Oh God, so they are,' said Raymund.

We had crabs.

A souvenir of France from the less than shiny double bed.

'Paint this on the affected area,' said the smiling chemist.

It was blue, not sky blue or deep blue like the ocean, more of a Wedgwood blue – not that any shade of blue is a flattering colour to paint your genitals.

We stood, freshly painted, on opposite sides of a paraffin heater and picked off small crustaceans, which exploded with a tiny pop as we dropped them on the hot metal top.

'This is fun,' neither of us said.

Nor did we say, 'One day we'll look back on this and laugh.'

I think the worst thing was writing to tell Stella, a lovely nurse I'd known in Bristol, who had come up to London to visit me at Raymund's and we had spent the night in Australian Helen's room while she had been away. She was one of the sweetest girls I ever knew and probably the last person I would have wanted that to happen to. But she was a nurse, so she probably could have got the blue stuff for free from the hospital dispensary.

'Still,' I said to Raymund, 'it could have been worse. We could've got syphilis.'

'You probably have to stay in a more expensive hotel to get that,' he said.

1962 – LOONY BIN No. 2

Once again, my stepfather put £100 in my hand and said, 'Go away.' So I went back to Paddington Station and looked at the departure boards again. Last time they had taken me to Bristol. This time, I went a bit further, down to Newquay in Cornwall.

The summer holiday season was a few weeks away and the town was waking up from its long winter sleep. The boarding house owners were back from their winter holidays in the Canary Islands. The canvas awnings were being pulled down over the shop windows and, like everything else in town, being dusted off and repaired. Hinges had broken, mice had eaten their way in, insulation had crumbled in the salt air and fuses had blown.

All around Britain, dozens of seaside towns like Newquay were waking up. There's a great atmosphere in those places out of season. The sea-fronts were deserted. The little stalls selling ice-cream and rock still had their boards up and the deckchairs were piled up under a canvas. It felt wonderful.

Most people were indoors, relaxing, polishing the silver and having a last cup of tea before the deluge. It had a timeless feeling that never changes. I was a bit too early for hotel work but there was a little old theatre a few streets back from the front so I tried there.

My timing was perfect. The two little old owners had arrived the day before and were setting things up for the summer season. I told them I'd worked backstage. I hadn't, but it wasn't the sort of job that wanted references so they took me on. I was the stage manager. I was also the assistant stage manager, the lighting engineer, set builder and painter. I was, in fact, the entire backstage staff. The pay was the lowest I'd ever earned but I doubled my wages by cleaning the theatre every morning.

Ronnie and Dickie, the husband and wife who ran the theatre, were both in their seventies and had been in 'the business' all their lives. If they had had any glory days, they were long behind them, as were those of most of the acts in our Old Tyme Music Hall show.

Ronnie and Dickie's claim to fame was that they had discovered two minor comedians who had passed their prime twenty years ago. Their framed photos were on the office walls with those of a hundred other hopefuls whose lights had burned for a few moments and then gone out. Hopeful faces in posed studio photos, signed with a flourish *'To Ronnie and Dickie with love.'*

It was beautiful, because all of them had followed their dreams and, at least for a while, they'd had fire in their hearts.

The theatre had regular places around town where their staff and performers stayed. So for the summer season of 1963 I was the staff and I was given a room in the house of a hoarder, not just any hoarder but one of unbelievable eccentricity who had elevated it to a fine art.

My landlady was seventy-eight years old and ran a tiny antique shop in town. She sold tiny things in her tiny shop and her house was full of them, not just them but everything that had ever come into her hands in the previous seventy-eight years.

My room, downstairs front right, was OK, but the rest of the house was unbelievable. I shared the room with Colin Reynolds, the gay ventriloquist in our show. To reach the bathroom upstairs, we had to inch sideways up each stair squeezing past fifty years or more of newspapers piled so high that they were forever collapsing. The simple act of going to the toilet could take half an hour by the time you'd piled everything up again. I threw a fish and chip wrapper in the dustbin one night and in the morning it was back in the kitchen, folded tidily on a pile of other wrappers.

All the other rooms were the same, a tiny walkway into the middle of the floor surrounded by mountains and mountains of stuff.

It wasn't all rubbish, I think there were priceless antiques here and there, but value had nothing to do with it. The chip wrapper was just as important as the Chippendale chair and the Japanese netsukes.

Getting the theatre ready for opening night was hard work and we were there seven days a week, but it was so exciting. The show people were lovely and I felt as if I had become part of a big family.

Most of the cast were old enough to be my parents or even grandparents, but that was all right. Lucy the soubrette was the only one the same age as me. She was the only one who could possibly move upwards, the only one who had any chance of her dreams coming true, but Lucy was only playing. When you're as rich as her family you tread water until you get married, then you pay other people to tread the water for you.

The rest of the cast had had their good old days. The photos were in the scrapbooks and they were waiting for the day when they'd retire to the bungalow by the sea, maybe in Newquay. Some of them should have retired already but it was in their blood like an addiction. It wasn't that they were still hoping for the big break, it was just that they couldn't let it go.

I could see why.

THE FAMOUS
CITY VARIETIES – LEEDS

6-15 ♦ MONDAY, MAY 9th, 1960 ♦ 8-15
Matinees– Tuesday & Saturday at 2-30

Telephone–30808

Manager & Licensee–Pip Pawson, 25, Moynihan House, The Flats, Leeds 9.

"LA FOLIES FRIVOLITE"

RAVEL
CLOWN OF CLOWNS

CHRIS
MARTIN
SENSATIONAL RECORDING STAR

BONNIE
DOWNS
BONNIE AND BRIGHT

FABULOUS
STRIP
SENSATION
KIM
FOSTER

THE
PATTON
BROS.
RADIO'S COMEDY TEAM

SANDRA
& DIANE
SPECIALITY DANCERS WITH A DIFFERENCE

COLIN REYNOLDS
THE YOUTHFUL VENTRILOQUIST

George Allen (Printers) Ltd., Brimington, Chesterfield.

This poster is not from the theatre in Newquay, I haven't managed to track one down for there. As you can see, it's from the much more famous City Varieties in Leeds, two years earlier, which is still in business today. But there at the bottom right is the ventriloquist – Colin Reynolds the Youthful Ventriloquist, who was in our show in Newquay and with whom I shared digs. Also, top left is Ravel, Clown of Clowns who is probably the same Alfie Ravel who was in our show, though I'm not sure about that.*

There was something so addictive about the whole thing – sitting in tiny damp windowless dressing rooms, putting on the make-up and the costumes and going out to entertain people who expected so little they would love you no matter what you did.

Just the smell of the Leichner greasepaint and the few seconds of anticipation before walking out into the lights seemed so wonderful. Not that I walked out into lights, but I could still feel their excitement. I could see why people like Ronnie and Dickie would go on until they died.

We did three shows, two performances of each a week plus an afternoon matinee, in a cycle. It meant that anyone who was in Newquay for a week's

* Thank you very much to Leeds Library and Information Service for permission to use this poster.

holiday could see all three shows, and lots of them did. We were nearly always sold out.

The shows were really corny, but that was their charm. Our audiences were solid working-class families from the North of England. They were on holiday and they wanted a good time, something where they always knew what was coming before it did.

They wanted comfortable slippers and songs they could sing along to and that's what we gave them.

In one of the shows I did end up walking out into the lights. It wasn't supposed to happen but I made a mistake and everyone loved it. We were in the Canadian Rockies and a Mountie was trying to rescue a girl tied to a railway track before the train killed her. I was the train, a wood and canvas cutout with me hidden behind it blowing cigarette smoke up a plastic pipe to the funnel. As I pushed the train across the stage one night, I dropped it and it brought the house down. I was standing there bent over, puffing away on a fag. They cheered so much that from then on I had to drop the train every time.

I missed Susan, but it was Edna I dreamt of. We had been so close to being perfect. I hoped she was at peace.

Sue and I had loved each other and nothing had happened to change that except my brain had taken me away into a world of its own – swapped young dreams for blank walls. Edna was surround by the same walls and when we were together we were in the same room.

I suppose I should have missed my daughter Charlotte too, but the amount of time we were together had been so small. It's terrible to think and say, but the rare times we saw each other after Susan and I separated, we were strangers. I looked at her and she was just a nice little child, not part of me that I could be close to.

Oh Edna, how I missed you.

Summer passed.

The show went on. All the shows went on.

I was so happy in the heart of my big new family.

But then, when I woke up one morning, the old friend was back inside my head. It was still dark outside and I lay perfectly still like you do when you know you're going to throw up and think that if you don't move it will go away, but all the time you know there's no way you're going to avoid it.

That's how I felt then.

You can't defy the laws of gravity. Once you slip off the edge of the cliff there is only one way you can go. I knew I couldn't escape, but life was so lovely in the theatre and I didn't want to lose it.

Not now, please. I'm happy now. Please leave me alone, I begged into the darkness.

Please don't come back. Get out of my head, leave me alone. Please, just for now, please. Let me keep this, the theatre and my lovely new family. Six more weeks and the show is over. Everyone will go their separate ways, then I'll come back into your dark caress.

But of course, it doesn't work like that.

I went back on the Librium I'd managed to live without since leaving Springfield, but it wouldn't work any more.

The arms of despair reached out and I couldn't fight them. I just wanted to be there in the theatre, in my little world behind the stage, pulling the ropes, dimming the lights, feeling there were people who cared about me, even if in a few weeks' time we'd probably never see each other again.

Oh fuck, is it going to be like this forever? If it was, I couldn't face it.

Colin Reynolds sat down beside me.

'Do you suffer with depression?' he said and I nodded.

'I thought so,' he said, 'I have it too. Is it bad now?'

I nodded again.

He brought me coffee and said all the right things, not that there really are any right things people can say. The worst thing about depression is that you are totally alone. No matter who is there and no matter how much they care, they can never reach you. If they wrap you up in their arms, it can help, but you are in another place, a place where only you can go. You know you are not alone but the feeling is so strong it smothers reason.

Colin did not put his arms round me, but he said kind stuff that made my sighs less deep.

'What about the theatre?' he asked.

'I don't know.'

I told him how much it had come to mean to me, how I felt part of a big family almost for the first time in my life, how I didn't want to let anyone down, but he said it was OK. He'd do my stuff, the lights and the scenery changes. Everyone would muck in.

They'd understand.

There were others there who suffered with it too.

It's a curse of the profession.

I wanted to ask him if it got any better as the years went by but I was scared to in case it didn't.

Colin spoke to Ronnie and Dickie and they phoned a local doctor they'd known for years. He'd seen it many times before. It seemed it wasn't just theatre people who suffered more than most. Summer seaside towns attracted misfits to work in the hotels who had similar problems.

It was ironic that while the paying public came to town to laugh and play, to escape all the stresses they lived with for the other fifty weeks of the year, those serving them lived in twilight worlds of nightmares and depression. We populated a transient marginal world that could never rest or settle down.

I wanted to pour out my heart, tell everyone in the show how much it had meant to me to be there with them all, but I was too embarrassed. Colin Reynolds said he'd tell them.

He drove me to the doctor's. The doctor made a phone call and Colin took me to hospital.

I'd been put in a time machine, and travelled back to the nineteenth century out on the moors in the tiny town of Bodmin at the Cornish State Asylum. That was what it said on an old brick wall hidden behind trees at the back of the place. It was called St Lawrence's when I went there, but it felt like the Cornish State Asylum. Springfield had been in a large city. It was surrounded by endless streets of suburban homes, part of the city itself, but Bodmin sat alone, a little one-street town in the middle of bleak moors. The street came in at one end and left at the other as quickly as possible. It was one of those places that made you wonder why people ever built a house there in the first place. Thick mists forever rolled across the treeless land, turning the place into Wuthering Heights. *The Hound of the Baskervilles* was set on these moors where people went crazy and no one noticed. The moors were the world stripped bare of beauty, a place where winter snows could kill travellers and wild ponies eked out an existence sheltering behind old stone dykes.

The mental hospital was a place to escape to, not from. Bodmin was the perfect place for it. If land itself could have an emotion then Bodmin had depression.

It was the same as before, lying in bed in the admission ward, the blackness holding me in endless despair, the brain an unfocused mass, dead from the neck up, dead from the neck down, adrift in a haze of Librium. Was this how it was going to be for the rest of my life, good months then bad months forever and ever?

Could I mark it on the calendar, putting part of each year aside for it for all the years to come?

I couldn't stand it. I'd give away the highs in an instant if doing so would take the lows too. The pills didn't work any more. They'd never killed the despair but they had stopped me caring. Now they didn't even do that.

I just wanted it to stop.

I just wanted to be normal.

There was someone ploughing the ward. The ploughman was eighty-five years old and had walked up and down the ward since breakfast behind his invisible horse. His arms hung by his side, his hands tilted to hold the reins on the tips of his fingers, his blank eyes fixed on the horizon to keep his lines straight. His horse knew where to go and when he had ploughed the forty-acre field he stopped, contented.

He had come out of a time machine. He looked as his father would have looked eighty years ago and his father before that – grey wool trousers too short above heavy leather boots, a wide black belt around the waist, a flannel shirt without a collar and a worn waistcoat.

He took his pipe out of his waistcoat pocket, filled it with tobacco from a leather pouch and lit it.

He had finished for the day.

Now it was time to eat, to read the Bible, then sleep. His son, also in flannel shirt and heavy boots, came to visit him. The old man sat in his bed. The son sat beside the bed. They smoked their pipes and didn't say a single word. There was nothing that needed saying.

An hour passed, the son looked at the clock, tapped his pipe out into the ashtray, put it back in his waistcoat pocket and went back to the farm.

The old man slept.

I had been here six days and this had happened six times.

In the bed next to me was the only patient younger than me. Kevin was sixteen, a local boy who couldn't stop interfering with the other local boys. He was asleep because they'd just given him shock treatment.

It was terrifying. I'd caught a glimpse of it being done it at Springfield, the man tied down with straps, his back arching like a bow when they pulled the switch.

When Kevin woke up he couldn't remember his name. This caused him more pain than anything he suffered before the treatment.

'It's Kevin,' I told him.

'Who is?' he said and then, 'But what's my name?'

'Kevin, it's Kevin,' I said, but he couldn't grasp it.

A week later he was back to his own version of normal.

He could remember his name. He could also remember that he liked to play with the genitals of small boys.

'Suck them like boiled sweets,' he said with a grin.

I went down the road and sat in the café drinking tea. On the jukebox The Animals were singing *We've gotta get out of this place.*

Bodmin was like travelling back in time to Charles Dickens. Motor cars down the street seemed out of place and it crossed my mind that you could probably go into St Lawrence's and never leave. You could become a nameless face, blending into the old brown woodwork. If you kept your head down, you could stay there until you died.

The Browncoats were like that. Old men in brown overalls dotted around the hospital. They had one thing in common and that was that when they were younger they had committed horrendous crimes. Now in their senile years they were considered harmless but all of them had spent years inside Broadmoor, a frightening prison hospital for the criminally insane. It was creepy knowing those little old men were once so dangerous. I found myself looking over my shoulder a lot.

There were a few patients who were locked away all the time, but mostly the ones who needed that had been taken elsewhere. There were hardly any young people there. It was like an old folks' home for loonies. They were out in the grass singing to the trees.

The young doctor suggested stopping the Librium, see how I went with no medication. I was nervous about it, even though it wasn't doing anything, but after the three-month sanctuary I actually felt OK. The darkness had almost moved off again.

Normal service would be resumed as soon as possible.

'I'm not sure there's much more help we can give you,' the young doctor said.

He was the first psychiatrist I'd met who seemed to live on this planet. He was certainly the first one who actually listened to what I said and I think he must have been away when they were teaching arrogance in medical school, because he seemed to care about his patients and even be prepared to admit there were many of us he couldn't help.

'You know none of us can really help you, don't you?' he said.

I didn't want to hear that but I'd always thought it was probably true.

'Manic-depression is something that only you can deal with,' he said. 'And most of the time that means learning to live with it. When it gets too bad to handle we can give you drugs, but you know yourself, they don't cure anything.'

I knew that, but he was the first person who had ever been honest with me and even though he told me everything I didn't want to hear, it made me feel validated.

'Though for a few people it does actually stop,' he said.

I so wanted to believe that, but I couldn't help feeling he was just saying it to make all easier to live with even though he said he wasn't.

'So I suppose it's time to go,' he said.

'Yes.'

'Back to London?'

I supposed so. The theatre in Newquay had finished for the year, so there was nothing to stay for.

'I'm driving up this weekend,' he said. 'Do you want a lift?'

I telephoned Aunt Pam. She said she'd love me to go there for as long as I liked and on Saturday we set off early in Doctor Keith's old Beetle.

I thought doctors earned good money. I'd have thought he'd have a better car than that, but he was young, probably no more than five years older than me.

I realised that in a few more years, I'd be talking to doctors who were younger than me. It took years to accept that. I'd always felt young and assumed that people in any position of authority or power must've been older than me, especially if they were bigger than me.

The moors were still covered with mist. Autumn was turning the little green they had into brown. The moors were one place I hoped never to see again. I thought I might like to see Newquay again, be back in the theatre the next year, but I was pretty sure that Ronnie and Dickie wouldn't want me after what had happened.

We drove slowly through the fog, half-expecting some creature draped in tattered bandages to stagger out of the gloom, but the only thing that happened was that we half broke down. We didn't actually stop but our progress was accompanied by a lot of coughing and uneven noises from the engine behind us. We limped into a small village and pulled up at a petrol station. It turned out one of the spark plugs had failed and we had been running on three cylinders. That seemed to sum life on the moors up perfectly.

The plug was replaced and we set off again. We crossed into Devon and the sun was shining. We stopped at a roadside caravan for tea and bacon sandwiches and I tried to switch my brain over from being inside hospital to being outside again.

The doctor asked me what I was going to do and I realised I hadn't given it a thought. I really didn't have the faintest idea. I'd stay with Aunt Pam and Uncle Ted for a while, maybe I could work for a bit in Uncle Ted's laundry until I decided where I wanted to go and what I wanted to do.

'How about working from the basis of who you'd like to see the most?' the doctor suggested, so I told him about Edna and how I couldn't get her out of my head. I also told him about Susan and our baby Charlotte, and how I felt guilty about what I'd done to them, how my depression had wrecked it all and that I felt bad that Susan didn't come into my mind the same way Edna did.

I didn't know if Edna was still in Bristol or even if she was still alive.

'Maybe you could find out,' I said. 'You're a psychiatrist, surely they'd tell you? You could get in touch with Springfield, they'd know what happened to her.'

He wasn't too keen on this idea, but I pleaded with him and he said he'd make enquiries on Monday.

'You know, there is a place that might do you some good,' he said. 'It's run by my old psychiatry lecturer.'

'Another hospital?'

'No, it's different,' he said.

He said it was a special unit where everything was run by the patients and staff together. It was all done in group therapy with everyone talking about their problems to everyone else.

'They have to vote you in,' he said. 'There are only about thirty patients and they're all about your age.'

I wasn't sure. I thought I'd had enough of hospitals for now but he said it was tailor-made for people like me.

Did I really want to go to a place with twenty-nine other manic-depressives all talking about how terrible it was?

I knew it was terrible.

'What have you got to lose?' he said. 'You can always leave.'

I suppose.

We talked about other stuff, our childhoods, girlfriends, school, what music we liked and what music we didn't like.

Then we were into Wiltshire and everywhere was thick with autumn trees and comfortable money. After the bleakness of Bodmin Moor, it was beautiful. We passed small villages full of the sort of cottages Susan and I had dreamt we'd live in one day. There were people about and I watched them enviously as we passed through their peaceful worlds.

It was hard to imagine anyone there having any problems at all, but of course they did. We must have gone by houses where there were marriages falling apart, children screaming for no apparent reason, people about to lose everything through the bankruptcy of a dream that had once seemed perfect, and of course people with mental illness.

For all its power over everything, mankind is the frailest species of all. We reached Surrey and my doctor delivered me to my aunt and uncle's door. They were so welcoming – the only ones in my family who never passed judgement and I felt safe and happy to be there.

They had always been the closest thing to a normal family in my life, mother, father and four children. Soon this would be changing, two of my cousins were on the verge of marriage and over the next few years the other two followed and the generations all moved up one.

But that week it was just like it had been when I was a child visiting in the summer holidays. The eldest, my cousin Stephen, twenty months younger than me, was going to marry a divorcee with a child in three weeks' time. I shared his room like we did as children and we talked about the old days, all the different places they'd lived, which places we'd liked best and the things we'd done.

The memories were close enough to remember all the details, but not close enough to bring sadness at their passing. Yet, now we were old enough to have some old days, and when we talked about them, they became good old days.

The Good Old Days.

That was the name of the show at the theatre in Newquay.

On Monday afternoon the doctor rang me. He said I had to go for an interview at the unit his old lecturer ran in two weeks' time.

'And Edna? Did you ring Springfield?'

'Yes, I did,' he said, 'but there's nothing I can tell you. When she left, they lost touch with her. They didn't even know she'd gone down to Bristol.'

'Oh.'

I asked him if he could ring the hospital in Bristol where they took her when she took all the pills, but he said there was no point, they wouldn't tell him anything. I knew that wasn't true, but I knew I couldn't persuade him.

I spent the next two weeks at Aunt Pam's. Sue brought Charlotte down to see me, but I had become a stranger to her. She looked at me and burst into tears. Sue and I were sad together. We talked about little things that would have no effect on us. I told her about Newquay and the theatre and the gay ventriloquist who did an act with a mop with eyes. I wanted to fall on my knees and beg her forgiveness, not so she would take me back, but just to say I was so very, very sad and ashamed for having put her through so

much unhappiness, but the words just wouldn't come out.

Maybe if I could have talked more, we could have struggled through the worst of it and come out the other side. But it was too late then.

Sue and Charlotte went back to London and I spent my days walking along the canal at Byfleet trying to make some sense of everything. It all seemed so cruel, what had happened. I had been so good as a child. I had never answered back. I had never even wanted to answer back. I had tidied my room, learnt my tables except the nine times one which is still a problem sometimes. I had always cleared my plate and said my prayers, but I was still the child who was so bad that he had made his father go away.

POSTSCRIPT – 2
HOW DO YOU CURE DEPRESSION?

How is it that some people can go through terrible times and come out apparently unscathed, while other people have no visible hardship yet fall into deep destroying depression that takes over their whole lives?

By depression, I don't mean the obvious depression brought on by the death of a loved one or some other bad event. They have obvious explanations. I mean the type of depression that seems to creep up unannounced.

Why does that happen?

Are we so poorly designed and evolved that this dark illness can just take us over and there is nothing we can do about it?

HAIR

In 1958 when I was 16 and an Art Student, I threw away the Brylcreem and grew my hair. It crept down until it covered half my ears, which was enough to make old ladies cross the street.

'My husband did not fight in the war for this sort of thing,' one of them shouted at me, and advised me that a good spell in the army killing foreigners would put me back on the straight and very narrow. I opted for the hair.

It never reached my shoulders, but even like this it was enough for strange men in raincoats to try to pick me up.

It was our duty as Art Students to rebel and it was so easy in those days – no haircut for a few weeks, tight trousers and a bit of rock and roll was all it took to piss society off. People rallied on TV predicting the end of civilisation. It was wonderful.

But then, in 1962, as the Beatles took over the world and even old ladies grew to like them and, for goodness sake, bank clerks grew their hair, it lost its shock value and appeal.

My generation became wet and weak. They grew their hair even longer, but they wove flowers into it, and turned into feeble watery middle-class protesters called Donovan.

The last bid for freedom was Punk in the mid-seventies, which produced my favourite band, The Ramones, but even that has faded away.

But then, of course, true rebellion is inside your head not your wardrobe.

1965 – LOONY BIN NO. 3

I was standing in the middle of a room. It was four o'clock in the afternoon. Everything felt gloomy – a typical British overcast day. Around the edge of the room was a single line of about sixty chairs and in every chair was someone I'd never seen before. Some were sitting silently in their own spaces remote from it all. Others were talking to each other in ones and twos. Some were my age, some older and most of them were looking at me. On my right, the half-greyed out afternoon sun tried to shine through four windows. It stopped halfway across the floor a few inches from my feet, unable to come any further into the room. In the second wall, dark trees masked the view from four more windows, trees planted to hide the hospital from the outside world, out of sight out of mind, though as it was a mental hospital, out of mind out of sight would have been more accurate.

Behind me there was a wall with a door. The fourth wall was empty. All the walls were painted hospital green from the floor up to a narrow black line that ran round the room at the same height as the sitters' heads. It looked like everyone had a ribbon in one ear and out the other, tying them all together.

Was this what I wanted, to be tied to all these strangers by a ribbon through my brain? Was this really going to help me in the slightest? Some of the faces looked weird. There was a man with one arm rolling a cigarette. Nowadays people become famous with less talent than that. Above the line the walls were hospital cream, that institutional gloss paint that chips to show pale blue and grey and black and finally cement.

The floor was grey linoleum, a patternless pattern designed to hide a multitude of sins. I was standing right in the middle of the room and I felt sort of scared. I turned my head from side to side. I could see about thirty of the faces and it was impossible to know who was who – staff or patients. They were all here, the entire population of the unit. They were all so white as if they never saw the light of day. I wanted to go now before it went any further. There in the sea I saw a nice face. Maybe I could hide in her arms. I tried to concentrate.

So, I was standing in the middle of the room.

'Welcome to The Henderson,' a man's voice behind me said. 'Perhaps you would like to introduce yourself.'

I turned my head but he'd stopped talking so I couldn't tell who it was. Was it him, the one with the clipboard?

'I…'

I was standing in the middle of the room and I seemed to have been struck dumb.

'Yes?'

It hadn't been the one with the clipboard. It was the thin one three seats down. He looked like a patient.

'My name is Colin.'

'Hello, Colin,' said a woman. 'Would you like to tell us why you're here?'

Couldn't. Wanted to but couldn't.

'I…'

'It's OK,' said the thin man. 'You can say whatever you want to here.'

'I'm, I'm…' So fucking tongue-tied. I did want to say but I couldn't.

I suppose I'd spent too long in places where you didn't talk about it. That meant everywhere but there.

Say that. Go on.

'Too long in places where you don't talk about it,' I said.

'Oh yes,' said a woman.

'Not here,' said the thin man. 'We want you to talk about it here.'

'That's the reason for coming here,' someone else said.

Oh fuck, it felt like I was in some religious cult.

'Come on,' said the thin man, 'tell us why you want to come here.'

'I thought it might help,' I said and I did think that, but saying it sounded so feeble.

'How?'

'The other places just fill you up with pills. Nothing changes,' I said.

Then it started coming. I tried not to look into anyone's eyes. That made it easier.

'The pills make you feel better,' I said, but then I added, 'No they don't, not really. They just make you dead, take away your feelings. You still feel the same, but you don't care. You don't care any more because it's stopped hurting. It never gets any better.'

A lot of people said yes, yes, yes, but my heart was beating. What the fuck should I do with my hands? They were hanging at my sides, nothing to do with me.

'I'm so tired,' I said.

My confidence began to fade then. I wanted to sit down. I wanted to leave. I wanted to be back in my room curled up on the bed.

The sun moved across the floor, creeping away from me.

Oh fuck, what am I doing here?

'I don't know what I'm doing here,' I muttered.

'None of us do,' said a woman mistaking my simple confusion for something deep and meaningful.

Brown hair, dark eyes. So beautiful, beautiful like it makes your heart ache. My focus slipped further and she looked right into me.

Oh God, I married you once, or someone just like you.

It seemed so long ago, but I was only twenty-three, so it couldn't have been.

'It all went wrong,' I said, but I'd lost them, not lost them like they were no longer listening but lost them like I'd gone somewhere else and mislaid them.

'Thank you,' said a voice.

'What?'

'Thank you.' It was the thin man again. 'Can you send the last person in?'

In the corridor there were six of us. We sat on a row of chairs the same as the ones inside the room, black metal, plastic seats with the pattern worn off. Mine had a tear in the edge. Someone had written on the plastic with a biro, but I couldn't read it. The walls were the same colour too so now the black ribbon went through our heads. Four other people had been in before me. The sixth went after I came out.

It felt like sanity gone mad. This was the only audition I'd ever done and I was applying to join a lunatic asylum. A girl two seats down was weeping but we all pretended she wasn't. That's what you did. In an office by the entrance two people were having a normal conversation – normal family problems, shopping, dinner and unpaid bills. I couldn't remember if I'd ever had a conversation like that, but I knew a lot of people who had.

The sixth person came out again, but instead of sitting down on his chair, he left. The door swung behind him, letting in the noise of a passing train. The door had disturbed the air. Now the dust danced frantically in the sunlight like little tornadoes. We waited. The crying girl was still crying.

One by one we were called back into the room. I assumed they'd been talking about us while we were been waiting, the staff and the other patients on their sixty chairs, voting who was in who was out.

But no.

This was nice middle-class democracy. So I stood in the middle of the room and they voted.

I think the thin man said, 'Who thinks we can help Colin?' but he might have said, 'Who thinks Colin can help us?'

I can't remember, but I was in. Most people wanted me. It was the first time in my life so many people had wanted me. I didn't want to look at the beautiful girl. I didn't want to see if she had her hand up or down. I looked. She had her hand up. The thin man didn't.

'OK Colin,' he said, 'we'll see you on Monday.'

'Thank you,' I muttered.

I had just thanked them for letting me into the asylum. I suppose that alone was reason enough to be there. As I went home, I still couldn't take in what had just happened. I sort of thought the place might help me but it was all so surreal. I had actually turned into a character in a bad 1960s BBC television play. I'd passed the audition and got the part.

1965 – LOONY BIN NO. 3 – PART 2

So I became one of the people sitting round the room while new people came and asked us to let them in. It was weird. Talk about the blind leading the blind, but on the other hand, who better to judge the blind than the blind?

On that first Monday morning in The Henderson, they took all my pills away. No one was allowed any medication, or rather no anti-depressants or tranquillisers or sleeping pills. If you broke your arm, you might get an aspirin.

Three people had left the week before. So now there were three vacancies.

A man was standing in the middle of the room and I took an instant dislike to him, though it was not so much dislike as fear. I didn't know why, but there was something about him that made my flesh crawl. He looked ordinary enough – jacket, jeans, clean, everything there, but there was something about him that was menacing. I think it was around his eyes. They stared out in a terrible lifeless way. I'd seen lots of people with lifeless eyes in those places, but they were people who had retreated into themselves. This guy's eyes were threatening as if to say he'd make anyone who looked into them lifeless too.

I can't remember what he said, but I knew he wasn't telling the truth. There was a terrible air of danger about him and I knew that if we voted him in, it would end in a big disaster.

My heart was beating in panic and when he'd gone back out into the corridor I told everyone how I felt and discovered I was not the only one. Over half of us felt the same, some even more than me.

'If we let him in, someone will die,' said a girl called Mary.

'Oh come on,' said the doctor, 'I think you're just showing your own paranoia.'

'And I think you're trying to influence our feelings,' someone else said.

When we voted, we didn't let him in, but it still ended with someone dying because after we'd told the man no, he went out of the room, left the building, crossed the lawn, climbed the fence and sat on the railway embankment.

When the next train passed he threw himself under it. The trains deliberately slowed right down as they passed the hospital but he still managed to kill himself and we all felt relieved.

TESTING, TESTING, ANYONE THERE?

'I'd like you to go to the Tavistock Clinic,' my old Ealing doctor said. 'For tests.'

I think we'd given up on the tranquillisers by then. They'd certainly brought me no tranquillity. At best, when I was taking eighteen a day, all they brought was apathy. The three hospitals hadn't helped that much either.

'Tests? What do you mean, tests?'

I didn't like the sound of tests. It felt like the doctor was having one last go at mending me and, if I failed, they might put me in one of those double-locked wards where the world forgets you ever existed.

So I was scared and suspicious.

'Assessment tests, that sort of thing,' she said.

'Why?'

'I think it might help.'

'Help who?'

One thing had changed after three loony bins. I had become more assertive. I'd only just realised it talking to the doctor and I quite liked it.

I think what happened was almost all the other patients in hospital seemed so beaten down and so accepting of it and I ended up despising them. I could see how easy it was to become like that. It was the line of least resistance, a comfortable option that made me scared I could end up like that.

The group-therapy unit was different, worse really. There everyone wore their illness on their sleeve – no, not their sleeves, but written big across their foreheads like cheap T-shirts. Look at me, I'm schizophrenic. Look at me, I was abused terribly and have forty-three psychoses all of which are worse than any of yours. The self-pity and the pride in it was terrifying. It was like they had to make themselves important, to make themselves stand out in the world any way they could. And the worst thing was, most of them hadn't wanted to give up their illnesses, as if by doing so they would become ordinary and be thrown back into the sea of mankind where they'd be forgotten.

Now I was away from there, they all looked so pathetic and it made me determined not to end up like that, so my initial response to the Tavistock was that I'd had enough of all that shit.

Two hospitals and the unit, what had it got me? Breathing space, that was all, and now I was being offered a bonus-door prize.

Free tests at the Tavistock because the doctor said it was famous, a world-famous institute where famous doctors and famous scientists studied human behaviour, and it was a privilege to go there.

They didn't study just any old looney. You had to be recommended. It was a privilege.

What, like boarding school?

That was a privilege too. For that you just had to be rich, for the Tavistock you had to be 'interesting', and unless you were really, really interesting, you probably had to be middle-class too.

So, I thought, *Why not?* I didn't think it would be any help at all, but it might be interesting.

'I'm going to show you some patterns,' said the lady in a white coat.

She was about forty, dark hair and quite attractive in a hidden sort of way and her white coat was really, really white with four pens in the top pocket. We sat opposite each other at a table and I found it hard to look her in the eyes, so I did what I always do and looked everywhere else, especially her breasts and her mouth. I think you can tell a lot about people from their mouths. I suppose me looking at her breasts told her something about me.

'And I want you to tell me what they remind you of,' she continued.

What, your breasts?

I knew I was being flip, but I found it hard to take it all seriously. It was like when Jehovah's Witnesses come to the door. Your initial reaction is to scream 'Fuck off.' You know it's the most sensible thing to do, but you seldom do it, well not until you've wound them up for a bit.

'Why?'

'Well, er, different people see different things in them,' she said.

Well, of course they fucking do. So what?

'Yes, and?'

'Well your answers will help us decide how we can best help you.'

I couldn't do it. I sort of wanted to, even though a large part of me knew the whole thing was totally pointless. All I could see was ink blots because all there was on the cards were ink blots.

There must be something wrong with me, I remember thinking, but honestly all I could see was fucking ink fucking blots.

I think mankind is preoccupied with finding meanings where there are none, which is most places. Most things exist and happen simply because they can. There is no deep reason behind them. What there is, is what you see in front of you.

Life and everything connected with it seemed more and more ridiculous.

I think I'd known it since I was about eleven, but whereas it used to depress me, by my mid-twenties I had begun to see it all as a joke. We were both the jokers and the joke.

I really did want to find pictures in the ink blots, but all I could see was the ink. If I tried really hard some of the blots looked like bits of raw steak. When I told her that, it didn't seem to be what she wanted to hear, except she did like it when we talked about blood.

I think I was supposed to see proper pictures, nightmares or my deepest thoughts and desires or at least a butterfly, but I couldn't.

So I decided to just make stuff up.

'What about this one?' she said.

'A vagina.'

She liked that, got quite excited, wrote it down, crossed her legs and blushed.

'A vagina?'

'Yes.'

'And this one?'

They all looked like steak, though if I squinted a bit it looked like two lamb chops.

'A pair of buttocks.'

'Really?'

'Yes, but I'm not sure if they're women's buttocks or men's,' I said. 'Does it matter?'

'Do you think it matters?'

Oh, fuck off, amateur.

I looked closer.

'They're women's buttocks, a young woman's.'

I've pressed another button.

'How young?' she asked.

Careful, I don't want to be labelled a pervert.

'Fifteen.'

169

She seemed happy with that. And so we went on all morning. Jesus turned water into wine. I turned ink blots into buttocks, bums and breasts.

After lunch it was word association. The 'what do you think of when I say such and such' stuff. I wondered how far I could go before she'd realise I was playing games. Unless of course she was smarter than she was letting on, and guessed straight away.

The body parts had gone down well, so I stuck with them.

'Mother.'

'Breasts.'

'What sort of breasts?'

'Huge.'

'Father.'

Oh shit, bastard. She's caught me off guard.

'Banana.'

'Banana? I don't understand,' she said. 'Why banana?'

'They used to bring me out in spots.'

'And you associate that with your father?'

'No.'

I didn't associate anything with my father. I'd only met him once when I was nineteen. How could I associate anything with him?

But I wasn't going to tell *her* that.

'Never mind, I think we'll leave it there,' she said.

I've no doubt taking the piss combined with all the vaginas and buttocks earnt me a label of some sort. I wondered how many labels they had, how many subsections of depression they had classifications for. It was probably linked directly to how many new anti-depressants and tranquillisers the drug companies could come up with.

If it hadn't hurt so much sometimes, it would all have been a huge fucking joke.

The next morning I caught the train out to Stanmore.

Pete and his pregnant wife were living in a huge derelict mansion in a street of millionaires. They hadn't become squatters,

but Pete's father-in-law was a property developer and had bought the old mansion to knock it down and replace it with six executive homes, close to the golf course and station, and while the planning permission was being sorted out Pete and Jill were living there to keep real squatters out.

There's something comforting about a big city in the light of a new day. Everywhere is deserted. This was not a part of the city where people left for work on the edge of darkness. Those people lived in other places with narrower streets. Those people were already at work, cleaning the office floors and polishing the brass for the people of Stanmore, who were still asleep in their beds.

Pete and Jill were also asleep and I didn't have a key. I went round the back but everywhere was locked so I sat by the French windows and looked out across the neglected garden towards the golf course. In the thin layer of mist on the green, I could see a tractor moving silently across the grass. Someone from down the line was cleaning the golf course for the Stanmore wives.

Soon the old house and garden would be ripped up and thrown away. The house with its circular drive and dusty ballroom, the cedar tree sweeping down to touch the ground, the stone balustrades, the conservatory, the kitchen garden and the greenhouse would all be lost to six executive identical brick homes close to the local golf course and station with plenty of parking.

It was sad but I suppose when the mansion was first there, people would have mourned the loss of what had been there before that – just fields probably. I walked through the garden. It had no say in its future. Next week, next month, next year, the bulldozers would roll in. The walls would fall onto the ballroom floor. The floor would collapse into the cellar. The dust would settle and it would all be forgotten.

The once-glorious house would have been transformed into flat earth dotted with broken bricks and splinters of wood.

Inside the old greenhouse at the back of the house there were weeds growing in the benches. I remembered my grandfather's greenhouses, the one full of tomatoes and another with small sweet melons, each precious fruit in its own string hammock. They had seemed so exotic to me as a child growing up in the climate of England. My grandfather had been so proud of them.

'Too good for children,' he always said, and I never got to taste them.

Someone told me that if you punch out a window very fast and aim for a space behind the glass, you don't cut yourself.

'Make your hand into a tight fist,' he'd said, 'and look beyond it.'

Thinking about my day at the Tavistock with the fucking ink blots, I was ready for a bit of window punching. All the Rorschach and Freud stuff was just for them, for their compartmentalised theories. You were there to be fitted into the compartments, an ink blot being interpreted into a deep and meaningless case history, one of those 'oh yes, I've seen it before' cases – patient type Z3A with a touch of 14B. Z3A + 14B = medication P17.

Well, fuck medication P17 and fuck the theories. I'd had enough of being a piece in their jigsaws. I'd been holding my breath since my first week in Springfield.

Make your hand into a tight fist.

So I did.

It was true, I didn't cut myself, and I would never have guessed how good punching glass could make you feel, which was probably good otherwise I might have left a trail of broken windows all over the south of England.

It was fantastic, a great big release, a cathartic letting go, but above all it was fun.

I'd had enough of listening to people telling me stuff and half-believing it. It was time for what you see is what you get and yes, of course breaking the glass was a symbolic release, but I didn't think that until I'd finished.

Right then it was just a great feeling, because I knew breaking glass was wrong. Sure, I knew it was all going under the bulldozer next week, but it was still wrong, illicit, like sex with Susan before we were married and doing it while my mother had been drinking tea in the lounge across the hall.

I made each pane of glass into a picture frame and in each frame there was a face. I could see my mother looking empty and holy and my stepfather just looking empty. There were other faces too, but I can't remember who they were.

I went on until I'd punched out all the glass on one side and then Pete came out of the house with a big grin on his face.

'We've been watching you,' he said. 'I want a go.'

'Just close your hand tight and aim a foot behind the glass,' I said.

'Oh shit,' he said.

He just didn't have enough anger and cut himself on the first go, but my elation was catching and he tried it again. We raced each other to finish the job and then went inside for breakfast and sticking plasters. While Jill fried eggs, Pete and I sat cross-legged on the floor of the ballroom and smoked

French cigarettes and said how wonderful it would be to actually own the whole house and be able to live there.

The morning sun struggled in through the big windows that looked out onto the garden. It danced in our smoke and stopped halfway across the floor a few inches from our feet.

When you are young there is no future. What I mean is that you don't think about it, you just take it for granted. You will live forever. The future will always be there and there's so much to do today, why waste time thinking about tomorrow?

Then you reach an age when you suddenly realise you are not immortal. The age varies immensely. I remember being at Ealing Grammar School. I was fourteen and there were boys in my class who were already old men, boys who could tell you the square root of eighty-three billion divided by Tuesday in a split second, but if you'd put them in the middle of a field, they would've starved to death before they'd found the gate.

And you see people on TV who are in their forties begin sentences with 'Of course at my age…' I know it sounds unlikely, but realising I was not going to live forever didn't really hit me until my seventieth birthday. I had a hard time becoming seventy. It was over three years ago now and I'm still not happy about it.

Yes, I know – *tough shit mate…*

And anyone who says 'I have no regrets' is either a bloody liar, had a never-ending brilliant life or hasn't had a life at all.

I've had all sorts of dreams and still do, impractical plans that could have been turned into the future. The dreams varied a little – different places, different wives, different numbers of children, my father coming back, discovering half-sisters and brothers, but there were constants too – an artist's life in the country away from it all. I think I've sort of got as close to it as I'm probably going to and it's pretty good now.

Pete and I talked about it and I realised that I couldn't remember the last time I'd been intoxicated by the smell of turpentine or even held a brush. There's this wonderful book by a man called Joyce Carey – *The Horse's Mouth*. And a fantastic movie starring Alec Guinness, who wrote the screenplay, as Gulley Jimson, a crazy artist who lives on a barge in the Thames and paints vast wild murals on derelict walls. I was sixteen when the film came out and it was the most romantic and exciting thing I'd ever seen. I saw it seven times. I've got the book, got the video and if there was a T-shirt, I'd have that too.

And there I was staying in a mansion with big derelict walls and I could make the movie come true. I went back to my parents, got clothes and paints and brushes and moved into the ballroom, the largest room in the house with walls as big as my imagination.

Even when I stood on a table I couldn't reach the ceiling so I tied a paint roller to a long stick and painted bits of the sky. The bright blue threw light into the darkest corners. I started painting a landscape on the big empty wall opposite the door. No one knew exactly when the demolition was going to start so I had no idea how much I'd get done before we'd have to leave.

I painted fields, rolling down into a valley with a stream and, floating above the water on a magic carpet, a beautiful woman. I wanted to get someone to pose for me. Susan modelled for life classes, but I knew that was not a good idea. So my floating Venus was a photo from *Penthouse*, unreal and idealised.

And then we did know how long it would be before we'd have to leave.

Two days.

So I forgot the valley and decided to finish with some birds flying towards the windows, but the table I'd stood on had been taken away with the other bits of furniture and I needed something to stand on so I could reach the sky.

But then, who doesn't?

POSTSCRIPT – 3
HOW DO YOU CURE DEPRESSION?

I don't know. Some people never do and all I can think of in my case is that I got angry, though I'm sure it wasn't just that.

I saw the people in the group therapy sessions at The Henderson, each trying to outdo each other with greater and greater problems, everyone eagerly diving deeper and deeper into self-pity – hardcore career victims – and all I could feel for every one of them was contempt.

After the depression I'd been through that had wrecked my first marriage and driven me to attempt suicide, I should have learned tolerance and understanding, but these people were revelling in their misery, wearing it like medals. They didn't deserve pity and I despised them and also the idiot doctor who thought group therapy would bring them peace and him a place in the history books.

I couldn't feel sadness for them or pity for them, not even the one or two who killed themselves.

Maybe it was just a defence mechanism, but I wanted to be nowhere near any of them except Edna who I still couldn't stop loving.

Maybe there were chemical imbalances in my head that changed in my mid-twenties. I do know that it's only now, writing this, that I've ever thought much about it. After all, my depression had gone so why on earth would I want to poke around looking for it? I might have found it again, which was the last thing I wanted. Of course if I had found the answer, I would now be seriously rich.

PERFECT VISION

To be an artist or an illustrator, there are a few things that are good to have. I think the most important one is reasonable eye-sight. Of course, most vision problems can be fixed with glasses or, in extreme cases, Braille. I have something with a wonderful name – STRABISMUS, which I assumed was the name of a famous doctor, but isn't. Strasbismus is a great name for a squint. One of my eyes points up to the left and the other points down to the right.

Until I got driving glasses, I sometimes had to decide which road to drive down, the left one or the right one. I could have glasses that would fix this completely, but they would make me fall over every time I stood up. So I've got a compromise and the world is only a little bit wonky.

The other thing that's good to have is perfect colour vision.

I am red-green colour blind, but so is my daughter Hannah and she's got two Graphics Degrees. Mine is not so bad that I have ever been killed at the traffic lights, but I can't see any numbers in those Ishihara colour dot eye tests. An optician offered me colour-correcting glasses once. I'm sure they don't work and even if they do, there's no way I'd ever want them. I can just imagine looking at my artwork with them on and getting very depressed.

Being colour blind does have one big advantage. Many careers, most of which could end up with you being dead, were not open to me.

PICTURES OF HOME

COLIN THOMPSON

I think this is quite good for a red-green colour blind person.

MOTHER'S PRIDE

In all the time I knew her, my brain-washed Christian repressed mother only did one thing that I admired.

One summer, when Hannah and Alice were about seven and eight, my mother came up from Dorset, where she and my stepfather were living, for a holiday at Denton Fell.

She seemed to have put on a lot of weight and turned red.

'Are you ill?' I asked her.

'I'm fine darling,' she said and took off her coat.

'You look a bit feverish.'

'No, I'm fine,' she said, taking off another coat.

'Is it cold in Dorset?'

It was the middle of summer.

'No, it's lovely,' she replied, taking off a third coat, a cardigan, two sweaters and becoming a lot thinner.

'Granny, why have you got three coats on?' Hannah asked.

'I'm not going back,' my mother said.

My stepfather and I had never liked each other, so I admired my mother for leaving him, especially in such a cool way. On the other hand I had never liked my mother either and now she had just told us she had come to live with us.

And she did.

For a couple of years she had a big mobile home in our garden and then, thankfully, she bought a little house a few miles away.

POSTSCRIPT – 3.5
HOW DO YOU CURE DEPRESSION?

There is only one fairly certain thing about depression and that is that it nearly always passes. Medication might help it go quicker, but I'm not sure that is always true. In fact it can do the opposite. And I expect there are some depressions that do not come and go. I can only speak about mine.

Each time, the really bad bit usually went after about three months, and, I suppose, you learn to recognise that fact.

So really the only true unknown is the nagging thought – *When is it coming back?* Of course, each time it goes, you tell yourself it isn't going to, but there's always that little self-destructive voice laughing quietly inside your head looking for the little crack it left there.

I think I exterminated the voice because it hasn't been back for forty-seven years.

A MOTHER'S WIT AND WISDOM*
*There was actually NO wit and very little wisdom

Returning home with a bad dent in the back of my van after delivering pottery – *'There was a low wall and it moved.'*

1966 – WIVES –
PART 2

I was out for the weekend, out of The Henderson staying with my oldest friend Mike in his flat in Islington. We had been smoking a joint that afternoon, the first time since I was sixteen and, I think, pretty well the last.

It wasn't that it made me feel ill. It didn't, just a bit vague, like a sleeping pill that hadn't quite sent me to sleep. I couldn't see the point. My head worked much better without it and I thought, *If I need this to feel good, then there is something wrong in my life.*

There were and had been a lot of things wrong in my life, but smoking pot was not going to sort any of them out any more than Librium had. They both seemed to do exactly the same thing. You felt the same, but you didn't care.

Evening arrived and a party started.

'Hello.'

What? It was the girl who lived in the flat downstairs. I didn't fancy her but she had a fantastic reputation so when she asked me if I wanted to fuck, I followed her downstairs to her flat and we did and afterwards we did it again and went back up to the party and five minutes later she went downstairs with someone else whose girlfriend threw beer over him when they came back up and then I went down with her again because her reputation was amazing and true and afterwards we had beans on toast.

It was all changing though. I had friends with mortgages and wives and babies and careers. Soon the day would come when the wives wouldn't want me to visit any more, the strange guy who lives in the nut house and has to take pills, too risky with the baby there, never know what a crazy person might do.

Part of me wanted to be like them with the mortgage and steady job, almost like I had when I'd been with Susan and worked in the screen-printing studio. But now I was on the outside looking in, from another planet.

The girl from downstairs took her fifth bloke down to her sweaty bed. Mike said she'd start on the women when she'd run out of men. I wondered if she ate beans on toast with all of them? Had to keep her strength up, I suppose.

That evening the hospital seemed so far away.

So I sat on a bean bag and let it all flow over me.

I wonder who that lovely girl with the red hair is.

Downstairs came and sat next to me again, too drunk to screw any more. No, too drunk to make it back down the stairs to her flat, pissed and full of beans, not smelling too good.

'We could do it here, if you like,' she said.

'What, in front of all these people?'

'Yeah. Why not?'

But the redhead was looking at me and I was thinking I could fall in love with her. Suede miniskirt and wow she had lovely legs. Never been out with a redhead.

'Anyone want to fuck me?' Downstairs shouted.

Someone made a grab at her, but passed out at her feet.

I wondered if the redhead had a boyfriend. Bound to have. Then I saw she was with a straight-looking guy who looked like an estate agent. She was smart too, tidy hair curled under at the shoulders, tidy lipstick and Jean Shrimpton eyes. So she's not going to want to talk to me. Oh well, it was a nice thought.

And so it went on, like all parties did. People drifted away, some with the people they came with, some without, some home to plan their own personal nervous breakdowns, until finally there was just Mike and his girlfriend, Paula, Ben, Mike's one-legged flatmate, and his girlfriend and me drinking coffee and smoking dog-ends. Downstairs had passed out on the sofa and in the morning she cried her eyes out and staggered off to confession like she did every weekend.

But I couldn't stop thinking about the redhead.

I hadn't the faintest idea who she was, neither did Mike nor Ben.

So I went back to Loony Bin Number 3 for another week of group therapy, which was like mutual masturbation with everyone trying to have a better brain orgasm than the next person.

The following example is absolutely true –

We were the usual-sized group – ten patients, three staff and the girls were telling everyone how they had been abused by their fathers. Except, like always, these sessions became a competition.

'My father raped me when I was thirteen,' said the first girl.

'My father raped me when I was fourteen,' said the second girl, 'and I enjoyed it.'

'My father raped me when I was fifteen,' said the third girl. 'We did it lots of times and I had a baby.'

Game, set and match.

But it ended up being the only treatment I had in all three hospitals that did me any real good at all. The more group therapy sessions I went to, and we usually had a couple every day, the more I thought how self-pitying and pathetic everyone was.

I felt no connection to or sympathy for any of them and there were times when I should have, but I just despised them more and more and their oppressive air of defeat.

There is no fucking way I'm going to end up like them, I told myself and it sunk in and I got angry and it was wonderful.

Meanwhile there was next weekend. Downstairs was having the party this time.

I suppose it'll cut out all those stairs, I thought and I was right. I think she got through about seven blokes that night, but I wasn't one of them because the redhead was there and she seemed to be on her own.

'I wondered if you'd be here tonight,' she said, which was exactly what I'd been going to say.

As usual, I was suddenly shy, but we managed to find an empty bean bag in a quiet corner where we could sit down together and talk.

Her name was Heather. Last weekend's boyfriend was 'Oh he wasn't anyone.'

'Oh,' I said.

'But he's got a nice car,' she said.

I didn't have a car. I'd never had a car nor a licence to drive one and I was in an experimental psychiatric unit run by a lunatic doctor who wanted

posterity to canonise him, but I was planning to leave it next week and go back to stay at my parents' while I decided what to do next – is what I told her.

Probably not the best sales pitch, but it seemed to work, even when I invited her to lunch at my parents' the next day, where my wife Susan and our daughter Charlotte would also be.

'You're an idiot,' said Mike when I told him later.

He was right, of course, and I never expected to see Heather again. It seemed like a ridiculous waste of time even going down to Ealing Broadway Station the next day, but I did and there she was and she came to lunch with my mother, my stepfather, my wife and our daughter.

Having just written this I realise I have created the opening sequence of a sixties French movie. See, life does imitate art after all.

That evening, I took Heather back on the train to Islington where she had a room in the attic of a house in Canonbury Square owned by a rich arty family and she asked me to stay the night. I did, but that night we didn't make love.

I wanted to and I think Heather wanted to, but I sort of thought I shouldn't as a way of saying thank you for her coming unarmed to such a weird lunch. So we just squeezed into her tiny bed and slept wrapped up in each other.

The next night I was back in The Henderson, but after three more days I couldn't take all the self-pity any more and left.

Friday night I saw Heather again and that night we did make love and two weeks later we moved in together and bought a bad-tempered parrot called Milligan who hated us.

I became a student at the London School of Film Technique. One morning I left college and went along to the Law Courts in the Strand and got divorced from Susan. After which Susan and her new partner Marshall and I went and had a cup of tea and pie and I went back to college.

Meanwhile, Heather, who had just finished a post-graduate secretarial course, went to work as the private secretary to a Vice President of American Express in charge of European Banking. At twenty-two she was about twenty years younger than all the other vice presidents' secretaries and had a secretary of her own called Paula, who was Mike's girlfriend.

THEN WE GOT MARRIED.

This was our wedding day at Islington Registry Office. We were both in white and the beautiful bride was swearing a corduroy suit, which I had made for her on her sewing machine. Come on it was the sixties, the greatest decade EVER. Heather's dad wore his medals and shiny shoes. Heather's mum wore a flowerpot.

I think we were almost the only couple we knew who had not been pregnant on their wedding day.

And we were together for thirty years, one way or another.

You could be mistaken for thinking this is a shot from a trendy 1960s movie by Dick Lester, but no, it's Heather and me on our way to The Rising Sun pub in Islington, minutes after we got married.

No, I think it's me who is mistaken, because I reckon this actually is a shot from a trendy 1960s movie by Dick Lester, though I haven't got the slightest memory of it. On the other hand it could just be a photo of Heather and me after we left The Rising Sun.

After a year, I left film school and got a job at the BBC. I should have been an assistant researcher for a few years, a researcher for five to ten years, an assistant director for ten years and then when I was old enough to be completely disillusioned I could have become a director.

I managed to shorten the path to six weeks – it was amazing.

I was twenty-five.

We went to the Outer Hebrides to make a documentary about an upper-class twit who had left a dilettante life in Chelsea to run a huntin', shootin' and fishin' estate. Brian Lewis, the producer, said if I liked the man then I could direct the movie. The man was an idiot, still living off his mater at fifty, but I loved him deeply.

Every one of the five people in my crew was older and far more experienced than me, even the trainee sound recordist, but they were wonderful. They could have made my life a misery, but they didn't and we ended up with a really good programme.

The trouble was, the voice in my head had started talking to me again. It said I had made a big mistake marrying Heather. At the time, I didn't know why the voice had started again or where it had come from or what the mistake was.

Everything was fine.

It was better than fine, but there it was. I had to go.

So my friend Mike drove me to Heathrow and I flew to Mallorca, still not really knowing why.

I took the amazing train from Palma to Soller and then a taxi to Deya and walked unannounced and unexpected up Robert Graves's drive, because when I told an art's producer I knew at the BBC that I wanted to run away and write or paint or something and that I was thinking of going to see Lawrence Durrell because I thought his books were brilliant, he said, 'No don't go and see him, he's not very friendly. Go and see Robert Graves, he'll talk to anybody.'

That was true about Robert. He did talk to anyone and some of it I could even understand. I was put to bed in a room under his house and the next day lent a two-room cottage to stay in. In the meantime, I fell in love with Robert's wife Beryl.

Robert Graves, Heather and my impersonation of Peter Sellers doing an impersonation of an Indian actor. Also Beryl's dogs, Jote and Bolita, and a posh gel called Penny Cooke-Yarborough, who we used to call Penny Cook-Breakfast.

I wanted Beryl to be my mother because she seemed to be everything my mother was not. We became really close friends.

Then, I don't know why, guilt probably, I wrote to Heather, fully expecting her to tell me to fuck off. It never crossed my mind for a second that she would sell everything we had and come after me. But beneath the high-achieving private secretary there was a North of England working-class girl who said, 'When you get married, it's for life.'

My first thought was to run further away.

My second thought was – *I haven't had sex for a month.*

Naturally, the second thought won. Heather was ovulating the day she arrived and pregnant within hours. It never occurred to me that her timing might not have just been a coincidence. Nor did I know that she had deliberately stopped taking 'The Pill' the day I'd left her.

So we came back to England and I finally realised that I hated cities and crowds and I needed to live in a place where I could just go out of the back door and pee in the garden and wait while my dog came and marked the same place.

So we went to the beginning of this book to live in the eighteenth century, and we were together for about another twenty-eight years. Some of it was great. Some not, because I never truly believed I was ever really forgiven for running away.

1971 – BACK TO THE SUTURE

There comes a time for all dads when babies lose their charm, when mother nature can longer fool us into thinking sleepless nights are fun. One day we begin to notice a strange smell in the house that our paternal instinct made us ignore and we also realise that we are no longer the most important person in our wife's affections. Suddenly we are aware that our status has dropped to equal last place with the dog, unless it's a particularly cuddly dog and then we're out in the yard with the sparrows.

We've done our duty, made sure the family name lives on, so now it's time to get our lives back again. Of course, this happens every time a new baby arrives and every time we somehow forget all the bad bits and just remember holding our beautiful baby and how wonderful it was the first time they smiled at us. We forget that the smile was just wind and usually came just before they threw up down our best shirt onto an expensive art book.

After this had happened the second time, Heather and I agreed we needed to do something about it. We realised what had happened to us and wondered what to do to protect ourselves. There was The Pill, but an older and wiser friend gave us the answer. He'd had his two point four children and had a life that seemed totally together so he obviously knew what he was talking about. He had the answer: *Get a vasectomy*.

'Vasectomy?' I said.

'Yes,' said my friend, 'it's great. Best thing I ever did.'

Nowadays tens of thousands of men have vasectomies every year, but this was 1971. Real Men didn't do that sort of thing and there was very little information. Would I lose all interest in sex and begin to sing soprano? Would I take up embroidery and spend my evenings watching figure skating on television?

'No,' said my friend, 'it's just the opposite. You can't get enough of it.'

Then of course there was the really important question.

'Does it hurt?'

'Not much,' said my friend. 'You're in and out in fifteen minutes.'

'You mean, they don't use anaesthetic?' I said.

'Just local.'

'You mean, you see them doing it?' I said.

We were living on a tiny island off a bigger island off the north-west coast of Scotland. I had gone there, with a nine-month pregnant wife, to become a famous author and artist. Two years later with a second daughter born and overnight fame still a distant dream, it did seem like a good idea to have a vasectomy.

I also had a third daughter, Charlotte, from my marriage to Sue and I thought why should Heather have to spend years swallowing dubious chemicals or why should we lose the romance of the moment fiddling around with condoms, when for some small temporary discomfort we could avoid all that.

At least, that's what I told myself.

The trouble was that every time I thought about it, I got this image of two strong nurses holding me down while a doctor came at me with a pair of sheep shears, or worse still one of those gadgets they use to put rubber bands round sheep's testicles.

I imagined myself walking around two weeks later and suddenly my shrivelled up balls would drop off and slide down my leg into my wellies. After all, this was the Outer Hebrides where sheep outnumbered people hundreds to one, so rubber bands would be their sterilisation procedure of choice. I was certain that if I wasn't the first vasectomy they'd ever done, I would undoubtedly be the first one they'd done on a patient with less than four legs.

However, when we got to the hospital, I found that not only was I not the first but the surgeon liked to have his patients well and truly unconscious.

'But you're only twenty-eight,' he said. 'I'm not allowed to do it under thirty unless there's a sound medical reason.'

'I suffered with depression when I was twenty,' I said.

'That'll do,' he said and wrote *'Mentally unstable'* on the form. This followed me round forever as I moved from place to place and doctor to doctor, though somewhere along the way it got changed and misspelt.

Years later I saw my file and it said I had a *'Personality Disodre.'*

I'm not sure what a *Disodre* is. It's probably a specialist medical term.

That was it. I had no more excuses and no reason to be afraid. I lay back, closed my eyes and kept VERY still while a nurse shaved every hair from my body from my nipples to my knees with a cut-throat razor. The next thing I remembered was climbing very cautiously into the car and Heather driving me home. It was two days before I could bring myself to look.

Purple is not a beautiful skin colour. Many people would like to be a different colour – lighter or darker, but no one wants to be purple.

If you combine this genital colour scheme with the feeling of having a small porcupine down the front of your trousers, then you either belong to some weird fetish group lurking in the lower depths of the internet or you've just had a vasectomy.

For two weeks I walked around like a cowboy from a 'B' movie Western, very slowly and with my legs as wide apart as possible. But eventually the embroidery healed over and everything went back to normal and the time to see whether it had worked arrived.

'We'll send you a kit in the post,' the doctor had said. 'You just send a sample off to the lab.'

But they didn't send me a kit in the post. They sent me a letter, a letter inviting me to go to the hospital for 'a test'. For two weeks I was too embarrassed to even phone and make an appointment. It wasn't that I didn't like masturbation, far from it. It's always been one of my favourite pastimes. As Woody Allen says in that great movie Annie Hall – *'Don't knock masturbation, it's sex with someone I love.'*

Wanking is free and usually guaranteed to make you feel good. But this was the Outer Hebrides where the children's swings in the park were padlocked on Sundays. This was not a broad-minded forward-looking place. This was a place where having sex sober and with the light on was probably a criminal offence. And to make it even worse I was an Outsider.

I imagined being locked in a dark cellar in boxing gloves to perform the terrible sin of 'self-abuse'. There would probably have to be two doctors and a psychiatrist present to make sure I didn't enjoy myself. And, I would possibly be examined afterwards by an optician to make sure I hadn't gone blind.

When I arrived at the hospital a nurse, who had probably been turned down for a part in *One Flew Over the Cuckoo's Nest* for being too severe, handed me a plastic bottle and pointed me towards the gent's toilet.

'In there,' she barked. 'Sample, and I don't mean urine.'

Over the years, I have had recurring back trouble and it was probably the following half hour that gave it to me. Every man knows just how easy it is to get an erection. We even get them in our sleep and wake up with them every morning. When you're young, you only have to look at an almost any woman to feel something stirring. Anything that vaguely reminds us of sex will start us off. But there is nothing about a hospital toilet in the windswept Outer Hebrides that could turn anyone on. Grey linoleum, grey walls and toilet paper made of cardboard. I sat there with my trousers round my ankles freezing cold and overwhelmed with that what-on-earth-am-I-doing-here feeling that everyone gets at various times in their life.

I have a vivid imagination and I stretched it to its limits, but nothing moved.

And then I saw the magazine. Others had been there before me. It was rolled up and half-hidden behind the toilet. I imagined *Playboy* or *Penthouse* or at least *Vogue*. I saw beautiful women staring out from its pages and at last I felt something stir. In a strange sort of foreplay I waited before reaching out for my saviour. I took the lid off my plastic bottle in anticipation. Everything was going to be all right.

I picked up the magazine, shut my eyes and opened it at the centre page. And when I looked, there in front of me was the most beautiful caravan I had ever seen. I flicked through the magazine and there were dozens of them, pages and pages of caravans of every shape and size. I have never felt so deflated in my life. Whoever it was who had been there before me had the weirdest fetish I have ever come across. Sure, some of the caravans were well-rounded, some were big and powerful but even the happy smiling women of suburbia standing proudly beside them couldn't revive my withered erection.

As dusk was falling, I finally staggered out into the corridor with my little jam jar, almost too weak to stand and beginning to wonder if the old-wives' tale about going blind maybe had some truth in it. Everything was certainly a blur. As the sun set across a peaceful sea, I drove home down the empty winding roads in a strange trance. Arctic terns circled in the clear sky, sheep lay down to sleep and my left arm felt as if it would never work again.

But the operation had worked and for the next very long time I enjoyed, mostly, risk-free sex, or rather greatly reduced-risk sex.

195

Honestly, I was NEVER a hippy. We were very poor.
It was cold in the Hebrides and I made this very
warm jacket out of an old lady's squirrel coat.

DOGS – 1

This is Wallace. He was the best dog I ever had. He came to live with us on Denton Fell at eight weeks and lived until he was twelve years old. He loved everyone and everything except black handbags. He was the inspiration for the three FEARLESS picture books I wrote many years later.

The big picture is the cover of a tile brochure for three ranges of tiles Heather and I produced for a while. People loved them and we got great publicity in *House and Gardens* magazine, but they cost so much to produce that they were never a great success and we moved on.

ZEN & THE ART OF BUILDING

OR
HOW TO COMPLETELY RUIN YOUR BACK IN LOTS OF EASY LESSONS USING NO MORE THAN A READER'S DIGEST DO-IT-YOURSELF MANUAL, AND A FEW SIMPLE TOOLS.

Between 1969 and 1975 Heather and I changed a tiny croft house at 5 Hacklete, Great Bernera on the Isle of Lewis into a much bigger house with a pottery workshop and a granny flat. All we had to do was learn concreting, bricklaying, plastering, painting and decorating, carpentry, slating, tiling, plumbing, electrical wiring, how to shatter rocks with fire, how to stop the chickens eating the putty out of the new windows and how to fix the roof down to stop it being carried away by the Hebridean gales.

Of course Heather and I could never have done all this incredible building work without some slave labour.

And like all slaves the world over, when the sun got too hot, they wore their knickers on their heads.

Though after work they were allowed to relax in the Executive Swimming Pool.

1990 – WRITING

I went down to London with a shiny black portfolio like the ones what proper artists had and dragged my pictures round children's book publishers with no idea at all about what they actually wanted.

They were all very polite, but apparently what everyone wanted was colour and all my drawings were black and white, which is not surprising because, as you can see below, *I* was in black and white until I was over twenty.

And I am colour blind.

No one at all wanted black and white.

While I was in London, being rejected by the publishers, I went to an artist's agent too, which I think was part of a kindergarten school because it was totally run by very important little children, and the very important little children skimmed over my pictures and told me I was too old.

I was forty-eight.

So I went home and redrew this in colour.

My first coloured picture since I was a little boy.

Then I went back down to London and all of the publishers I had seen before were in a meeting except for a nice lady who worked for a publisher called Hodder and Stoughton in a rabbit warren in Bedford Square, where you went in through a front door, down into the cellar, through a door into next-door's cellar and then upstairs into next-door's hall, then up more stairs and more stairs to her office under the roof which, of course, was exactly the sort of place a children's book publisher's office should be.

She had probably missed the meeting all the other publishers were at because it would have taken her too long to get out of the building.

Her name was Linda Jennings and she looked at my coloured stairs and said, 'Very nice. Why don't you write a story?' Which sounded to me like, 'No, go away.'

Which I did – go away that is, not write a story.

But I was wrong because Linda Jennings kept phoning me up and asking if I'd written a story yet.

I think Linda Jennings had part-time deafness because every time I told her I couldn't write, she didn't seem to hear me.

After a few more phone calls, she got her hearing back because when I told her that time that I couldn't write, had never ever thought for a single second about writing and didn't want to do it anyway, she told me not be silly and just get on with it.

And she never told me I was too old because I think she was older than me.

Eventually, more to stop her pestering me than anything else, I sat down and wrote a story.

ETHEL THE CHICKEN

It was about 2500 words long and took me about two days AND to my great surprise it was much easier than I'd thought it would be and I'd really enjoyed writing it.

So I posted it to Linda Jennings, who said it was wonderful and why didn't I write another story and Hodder and Stoughton would publish them both the next year together on the same day.

'To start off your writing career,' Linda said, which was the first time I knew I was going to have a writing career.

So I wrote.

A GIANT CALLED
NORMAN MARY

It was all so easy at the time. It was only later I realised how incredible it was. But there are lots of things like that, things you take for granted when they happen because that's what you're doing at the time. It's only afterwards, when you've done them and have time to think about it, that you realise how fantastic they were.

Over the years, I seem to have been given lots of wonderful things because I was in exactly the right place at the right time.

Ethel and *Norman Mary* came out on the same day at the beginning of March in 1991. So now, seventy-five books later –

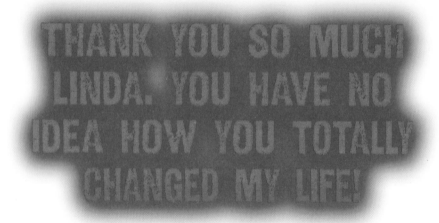

THANK YOU SO MUCH LINDA. YOU HAVE NO IDEA HOW YOU TOTALLY CHANGED MY LIFE!

Norman Mary is wearing a tie from my old prep school in Ealing – Durston House, which is still going strong (the school that is, not the tie).

GANDERS

Ethel the Chicken

COLIN THOMPSON

GANDERS

A Giant Called Norman Mary

COLIN THOMPSON

Since starting her career in 1991, Ethel the Chicken has been in eight other books and this first story is still in print in a collection of three books of short stories called 'WILD STORIES'.

A couple of years after Ethel first came out I saw this written in big chalk letters on a bridge in Carlisle – ETHEL THE CHICKEN WORLD TOUR. I never found out who did it.

OUTRAGEOUS SHOWING OFF

This is the first review I ever got. It came completely out of the blue from a lady called Margery Fisher, who was a legend in children's books in England and nine times a year for over thirty years published a magazine called *Growing Point*.

GROWING POINT

VOLUME 30
NUMBER 2
JULY 1991

Margery Fisher's regular review
of books for the growing families
of the English reading world
and for parents, teachers
librarians and other guardians.

Published by
Margery Fisher
Ashton Manor,
Northampton,
England, NN7 2JL

Six issues yearly:
post–free subscription £5.00
or single copies £1.00
(U.S. $12.50
or single copies $2.50)

Printed by
Davies Fleming & Associates
Round Spinney, Northampton.

In this issue:
Special Review:
Ethel the Chicken by
Colin Thompson
Voices of Adventure
Shifts and Balances in the Past
Caring for Nature
Other reviews and
shorter notices

SPECIAL REVIEW

COLIN THOMPSON *Ethel the Chicken* Hodder and Stoughton £4.95 Ill. by the author 44 pages 8¾ x 5¼ March '91 0 340 53107 X.

The current preoccupation with literacy, with 'teaching children to read', has led to a fashion for a fiction format in which text and pictures are more or less evenly balanced, so that apprentice readers, equipped with the power to translate letters into words but still deterred by the length and structure of a single extended story, could be encouraged by small areas of text and by a certain narrative tendency in the illustrations. Unfortunately many of these well-intentioned easy reading exercises are mismatched; either the texts are flabby and impersonal or the pictures are so grotesque and facetious, so nudge-nudge if you like, that they clash with more sober texts or blur the effect of verbal felicities. In particular, verbal and visual humour need to be carefully balanced if they are to capture a reader rather than puzzle him with counter-suggestions. When words and illustrations consort perfectly together, expressing both the warmth of humour and the tingle of wit, the result is a masterpiece and I think *Ethel the Chicken* is a masterpiece.

For one thing, it has a wonderful opening paragraph with an invitation to read on which would be hard to resist:

"At the end of a quiet street at the edge of the town stood an old empty house. Behind the house, at the bottom of the overgrown garden, in a wooden box hidden under a bramble bush, lived a chicken called Ethel. On the side of the box was a label that said FIRST CLASS ORANGES. Even though chickens are nearly as stupid as sheep, Ethel knew that she was not an orange.

The reassuringly simple shape of the story and its direction from start to finish are suggested in this paragraph, first with the box, which remains the focal point through the five sections of the tale, and then with the introduction of a personality, both as hen and as quasi-human being. Not that Ethel is a dressed-up animal; she may have, in the author's drawings, a rather knowing eye, she may even have a voice ('Wow, a talking chicken', an astonished ant shouts when he hears her chatting to the young rat Neville who finds her in her box but who is uncertain of her species) but she lays eggs, she eats woodlice and worms and she recognises the seasons as a fowl might. The humanity she has borrowed provides an emotional warmth. Forgotten after the death of an old lady who had brought her food and scratched her head, Ethel suffers from loneliness; children can sympathise with feelings which are only projected a little way out of that sense of absence and need which an animal might suffer, just as they can be glad with the hen when, after sitting out the winter, she rejoices in the children newly come to the house who discover her garden refuge.

The open sentiment of Ethel's situation is balanced by a dry humour in which you can feel the author's enjoyment of his own sly allusions and incongruities. The young rat is hauled off by his mother, who is no more able than he is to disregard the label on the box, with the reproof 'How many times have I told you not to talk to strange fruit?'. When the house is once more occupied Neville and his family move to a drain under a restaurant in the town — 'The rubbish is really great'. The illustrations carry over the easy, elusive humour as they show Ethel perched on a branch, a rat sampling a currant bun, the nice detail of a mouse-snowman beside the tracks of a robin; equally, in the pictures the house and garden, the incoming tenants, the flowers and snowdrifts, fur and feathers, are meticulously arranged and delineated, helping imagination and marking out for the sake of hesitant readers the onward march of the story. Symmetry, an apt selection of words, a judicious alternation of dialogue with description, above all a truly personal voice — here are enough merits to guarantee this compact book the fortune it deserves with the young and with their presiding guardians who, if they want their charges to become lifelong readers, must catch books like this on the wing.

1992 – MY FIRST PICTURE BOOK

MEMORIES – PART UMM . . .

We forget a lot of things in our lives, some of them are things we want to forget, painful things, bad dreams, enemies, but there are things we want to remember forever, but have also forgotten, nice things, happy dreams, friends. And we hang on to a few memories that we replay over and over again.

There's a lot of stuff you don't need to remember, like where the bathroom was when Edna and I lived in together in Bristol. All I can recall is that we had to go upstairs, but there isn't a single image I can bring back even though we always bathed together. It doesn't matter that I can't remember anything about the room, but I'd have liked to be able to remember the baths we shared.

I'm sure that every detail of our entire lives is stored in our brains. It's just that sometimes we can't remember where we put them. Some things will stay lost forever. Some might be there right next to something we're already thinking about and there are others that we trip over at the most unexpected moment.

And between the good and the bad memories is where most things are. The boring, the mundane, the exciting, the tiny and the life-changing all thrown together to be sorted out later.

Or not.

DOGS – 2

My daughters, Hannah and Alice, and I went to the animal shelter to get a kitten, but there was an outbreak of something so all the cats were in quarantine. As we left, we passed the dogs and sitting at the back of one cage under an infrared heat lamp there was this tiny little whippet puppy that had been left on a bus. We all agreed he was a MILLION times better than any cat. We spent the evening picking the fleas off him and called him Max. He lived until he was fourteen and now years later in Australia, I've got an almost identical whippet called Max. I think whippets are not created like other dogs. They are photocopied.

And this is the lovely stupid insecure Belle who was scared of moths.

SECRETS AND LIES

When I was a teenager, cool clothes were invented. One week, we had to go into department stores and buy our clothes off exactly the same racks our dads did. The next week, small bright shops appeared everywhere that our dads crossed the street to avoid in case the contents were infectious.

Even in Ealing we had one – Michael's Man Boutique – not a place to buy men, but a place selling trendy modern gear.*

In workshops behind these temples to youth, there were old Jewish tailors running the whole thing, while we thought the fab guys serving us, who were the same age as we were, had invented it all.

As if.

THE FINE ART OF SELF-DESTRUCTION

Over the years I've tried to work out why this self-destruction seems to have followed me. It ruined my first marriage. It helped ruin my second marriage and it ruined other wonderful things too.

The only conclusion that I've come to is that because I was brought up to believe it was my fault my mother had sent my father away, I had to be punished. So whenever things were going really well, they had to be wrecked because I had been such an evil child.

This might not be the explanation, but I can't think of another one.

The fact that I discovered when I was sixteen that my mother had brainwashed me with a complete lie doesn't seem to be enough to fix it.

I sometimes wonder if hypnosis could empty my subconscious of the guilt that my conscious knows is completely untrue. Probably not, I think it's too far in. But it would be interesting to try, though I've never tried it, but I suspect I'm one of those people who can't be hypnotised.

---

* Which was a new word that meant 'clothes'.

211

1994 DENTON FELL –
NEAR THE END

I was walking along the road to nowhere.

The dirt track went past my house into the middle of the forest, a dead end that just stopped. There wasn't even enough space to turn a car. Rows and rows of fir trees had been planted over what used to be the farm that went with my house. Even the narrow firebreaks that used to wander off the road like bright green ribbons had disappeared. The branches had closed in, the owls had moved away and the grass had died of darkness.

Of course the places the paths led to – the waterfall that vanished into the earth where a lake had collapsed into a coal mine a century earlier, drowning three men, the centuries-old ruin with its crumbling walls, the place where the badgers lived – were all still there, but now they were secret islands surrounded by the endless black sea of factory trees, lost like Aztec ruins until the forest gets cut down in thirty years' time. They became my secrets. I was the only person in the whole world who knew how to find them.

I used to like going to those places, knowing that I was the only living person who ever did. At the waterfall, you could still see the tree trunks the rescuers had thrown into the hole in an attempt to stem the flood and save their companions in the mine. A hundred years had passed since then, but the tree trunks were still there. I suppose the three skeletons were still down there too, trapped in waterlogged tunnels with their boots and pick axes. It's difficult to imagine how hard their lives must have been, hacking the coal out of seams no more than two feet high, that cut up through the rock at forty-five degrees. I found an old horse shoe nearby and once I saw badger's footprints but never a badger.

As the trees began to grow closer together, I used to chop the ends off the branches to keep the paths open, but it was a losing battle. Later I used to walk bent double beneath the branches, but eventually, I gave up and stayed on the road. The trees grew taller until you couldn't even tell where the paths had been.

It was four o'clock in the afternoon, overcast, the same as the day before. It was midsummer but it felt like winter, everything so gloomy, me, the weather, the past, the future. As far as I could see, inside and out, life and the world were grey, all the colour washed away.

Behind me there was a locked gate. I had a key but it was easier to leave it on its hook in the kitchen behind the sugar thermometer, and simply climb over. My three dogs had run on ahead through the gap I made for them in the fence. We'd been on this walk so many times, they'd worn away the grass beneath the broken rail. Last night something else must have crawled through their opening because today they all sniffed the wire and my whippet Max lifted his leg to reclaim his domain.

I wish I could have reclaimed my domain that easily.

Far away down in the valley I could hear the faint hum of traffic. Apart from that there was silence except for a skylark twittering above me, the poor bird after two weeks of clouds and rain, trying in vain to fulfil its destiny and pretend the sun was shining.

No one ever came up to Denton Fell. My house was the only building there. Before the trees were planted there had been fields of sheep surrounded by stone walls that had stood there for hundreds of years and on the far side of the valley you could see the remains of Hadrian's Wall and in the distance beyond that, Scotland. My house had been joined to other farms by winding lanes that led down to the village and on into the world. Now the sheep were gone, the walls that had been patched and repaired by a dozen generations were falling down, and the forest surrounded us like the barren emptiness of space.

It should have been paradise, my own world, seven green acres on the top of a hill, and it had been for over fifteen years, but it wasn't any more. When I had moved there twenty years before it *had* felt like paradise. I had found my own little world, but now it felt like a prison and each year the walls got higher and the real world seemed further away.

So I walked into the forest every day and hid in my dreams, the easy escape. It was a forest that had killed everything that had been there, until all there was left apart from the trees were a few nettles and a bit of scraggy grass reaching up to the light.

I remembered when the trees were no taller than pencils, there were rare plants up there, tiny orchids and a scrappy little shrub I was told only grew in two or three other places in the whole of Britain. There were short-eared owls too that hunted in daylight and there had been one fantastic day when I'd seen twelve all at once.

Now they'd gone, the birds and the plants, leaving the forest as a silent as a grave, cold and dead. My dogs ran through the gloom beneath the trees and came out confused, finding the only scents to follow were their own.

Once I'd had a head full of dreams that had the chance of becoming reality. They seemed to be gone too, all turned into daydreams, wild ridiculous fantasies that had no real roots in possibility, and as time passed, I spent more and more time in my daydreams and moved further and further away from reality.

Why had I married Heather? Thirty years we were together. At that point, that was more than half my life. She hadn't insisted on marriage. We could simply have lived together or apart and been lovers. I hadn't had to marry her, except of course I wanted to and she wanted to so we did. I have this deep-seated insecurity that needs to be married. Since I was eighteen I had only been unmarried for a few weeks. When I realised I'd made a terrible mistake and ran away from her over twenty-five years ago, why didn't I keep running? Why did I wait for her to come after me?

I'd run away from the gloom of London to the comforting warmth of the Mediterranean, never expecting her to follow me, but she had and I'd waited for her and the day she arrived she got pregnant, which I naively assumed as a coincidence. She hated the Mediterranean. Her skin, as white as paper, burnt in a few minutes and peeled away like the layers of an onion that I once actually wrote a letter to a friend on.

So we came back to the gloom of Britain and moved to the Isle of Lewis, back to her sort of climate. There were wonderful times, starting the pottery together, having two daughters, but there were terrible times too until eventually it seemed as if all wonderful bits were further and further back in the past.

The three-hundred-year-old paradise on Denton Fell, where we lived for twenty years and I had thought I would live in until the day I died, became a prison that became harder and harder to leave. Each year I said I would and each year I chickened out – too frightened to walk away into nothing.

As our lives grew colder and colder and further and further apart I asked Heather why she had married me.

'I thought we'd make a great team,' she said. I suppose we did for a while, but I'd rather she'd said because she loved me so much she wanted to spend the rest of her life with me.

Time passed.

Our daughters both left home for university and apart from a few holidays, they never lived on Denton Fell again. Hannah and Alice had been

the only thing that had kept us together and then they became the main thing we fought over.

There is a thing parents do called *splitting*, where the parents divide up the children. I was too naive to realise people did this and it wasn't until we had been apart for several years that it was explained to me. It just never occurred to me people would do that.

So I'd been given Hannah and Heather kept Alice.

Alice was taught to believe that I didn't love her and I fought hard with Heather defending Hannah against her persecution. Everything had become bitter and angry and broken and could never be repaired.

As I walked the dogs through the forest, I had ridiculous daydreams, all far-fetched, though I suppose the one with the aliens arriving in a spaceship and making all my wildest dreams come true was probably the most ridiculous.

There were no limits in my daydreams. I could have whatever I wanted, be whatever I wanted.

Why do the aliens never come when you really need them?

But then everything did change.

Forever.

Not aliens, but a class of year seven boys at a High School in Sydney, Australia, who had fallen in love with my picture book, *Looking for Atlantis.*

They wrote to me, raised the money for a plane ticket and invited me to visit them.

The day after I flew to Sydney, Heather went to a solicitor and they drew up an ultimatum that was ready for me when I got back. Several pages of conditions I would have to agree to if I wanted us to stay together.

I'm kind of curious to see it now, but at the time I refused to read it. I was leaving anyway, so what was the point?

Our daughters were twenty-six and twenty-four living their own lives out in the world. It never occurred to me that their parents splitting up would bother them that much and I was really surprised when Alice was so hostile. She hadn't lived there for a few years, but I had broken up the family home and no amount of apologies could make things right. We ended up not speaking for almost five years.

Hannah was cool for a while, but she and I had always had been closer so we never lost contact.

I suppose my surprise at their anger was based on my relationship with my own mother. I can honestly say that at no point in my life did I feel any

love towards her and when she died a few years ago I felt nothing, no sadness, but no release either. She was a selfish unthinking woman who gave me a lot of damage for which I could never forgive her, and the fact that she hadn't done any of it deliberately to hurt me, is irrelevant. It's the results that count, not the reasons behind them.

I have kind memories of my first wife Susan. She was beautiful and gentle and wonderful and I hurt her terribly with my depression. It destroyed our marriage. It was awful and I hope now that she has forgiven me.

No matter whatever might have happened in the future, Heather and I would never have been friends again. She was the angriest person I ever met and after I had gone she tried to spread her anger and hatred to all my friends and relations.

Finally, when she was fifty-five, the anger gave her cancer that killed her in less than six months. Only then did Alice and I become friends again.

THE BOOK THAT BROUGHT ME TO AUSTRALIA

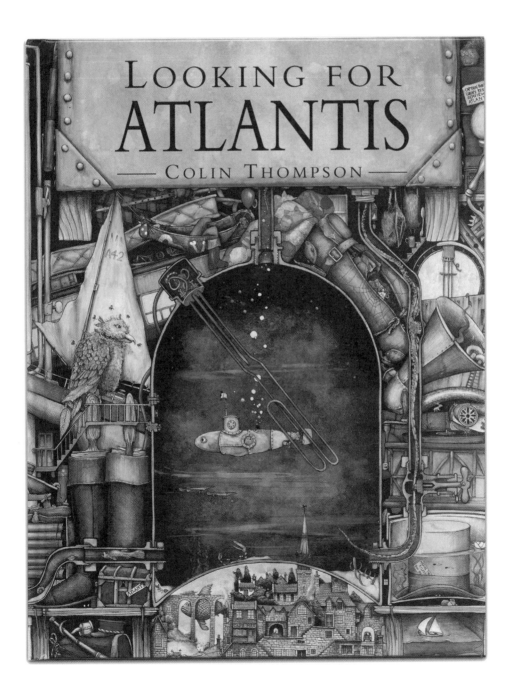

1995 – OVER THOUSANDS OF HILLS AND VERY, VERY FAR…

So I flew to Australia for a week to visit the school, and as I came through immigration where Anne, the teacher-librarian who had organised everything, was waiting to meet me, I fell in love.

Instantly.

The week became ten days while I tried to persuade Anne that a twice married, ex-mental patient thirteen years older than her was exactly what she needed in her life.

After ten days I went back to England to collect:

- more clothes

- my computer

- all my drawing pens and pencils

- some books

- some CDs

- and as much of my life as I could cram into a large station wagon*, which wasn't much, as I've realised many times over the past twenty years every time I've needed a drill or a hammer to fix something and had to go out and buy a new one.

I also got an AIDS test at St. Thomas' Hospital, which said I didn't have it, and my very first credit card. And then I gave Heather my half of Denton Fell, which was probably a bit impulsive even though I did get my grandmother's and mother's photograph albums in exchange.

The day after I drove down to London, with my much-reduced worldly goods, *my* mother, not Heather's mother, moved into Denton Fell.

Before I left England I discovered how many of my friends were living lives of quiet desperation and envious of what I was about to do. They said they would all have come too except every single one of them had endless reasons why they couldn't possibly come right now at this very moment.

---

*   *I realise now I should have hired a nice big van.*

'You are so brave,' they all said, 'just leaving everything and moving half-way round the world at your age.'

I was fifty-two.

But bravery had nothing at all to do with it. It would only have been brave if my leaving had been a question of making a choice.

It wasn't.

It was much simpler. There was no plan B.

It was just – *This is what I'm doing now.*

Back in Sydney, Anne kept asking herself if she actually wanted me to come back into her life, but fortunately I was much too far away to hear her.

So ten days after I'd left Australia I was back again. Now twenty years later and married to Anne, I'm still here and living in a valley that really truly is called The Promised Land.

So, I suppose I have found Atlantis and it's in Australia.

AND I AM, TO BE CONTINUED . . .

Colin tohmson
by Donald age 7   12·2·15

I have made preparations for the inevitable problems of old age.

Fianlly, I will go and live in the wisteria.

POST–POSTSCRIPT
HOW DO YOU CURE DEPRESSION?

By the time I reached twenty-five, my depression had mostly sort of gone. By the time I reached twenty-five, I knew that I would never fit into the mainstream. I couldn't go with its flow, nor did I want to and nor did I want to swim against it.

So I climbed out of the water and went to look for my own pond.

*I'm sure I've missed a lot of things out that every successful
book needs, so here they all are in one exciting recipe.*

THE 42 SHADES OF FREE RANGE CODE ORGANIC GLUTEN–FREE ANTI–AGEING HAIR–REGROWTH STAMINA WEIGHT–LOSS BEST EVER MINT SAUCE RECIPE*

INGREDIENTS
1 sweet and juicy apple – do not peel
1 mug of mint leaves
Malt vinegar
Caster sugar

Grate the apple into a blender until you reach the core. Add the mint leaves. Chop like crazy, but not into a puree. Put quite a lot of caster sugar into a small saucepan with some, but not too much, vinegar. Stir and heat just until the sugar has dissolved. Remove from heat and let it cool for a bit. When it's cool enough to stick your finger in, which I recommend, pour it into the blender and blend some more. Taste and add more vinegar (or sugar) until perfect. Pour over roast lamb, salad, roast potatoes, anything.

For a variation, try replacing some of the vinegar with cider – I haven't tried this yet, but it seems like a good idea.

---

* *Because every second book is a bloody lifestyle/cook book.*

224